A GUIDE TO
DEAF MINISTRY

A GUIDE TO
DEAF MINISTRY

Let's Sign Worthy of the Lord

■ ■ ■

DeANN SAMPLEY

Foreword by Joni Eareckson Tada
Illustrations by V. Duane Anderson

**Ministry
Resources
Library**

Zondervan Publishing House • Grand Rapids, MI

A GUIDE TO DEAF MINISTRY
Copyright © 1989, 1990 by DeAnn Sampley

MINISTRY RESOURCES LIBRARY is an imprint of Zondervan Publishing House, 1415 Lake Drive, S.E., Grand Rapids, Michigan 49506.

Library of Congress Cataloging-in-Publication Data

Sampley, DeAnn, 1954–
    A guide to deaf ministry : let's sign worthy of the Lord / DeAnn Sampley ; foreword by Joni Eareckson Tada ; illustrations by V. Duane Anderson.
       p.   cm.
    Includes bibliographical references.
    ISBN 0-310-52191-2
    1. Church work with the deaf. I. Title.
BV4463.S25   1990   90-30821
259'.4—dc20   CIP

Edited by James E. Ruark
Designed by Rachel Hostetter

Printed in the United States of America

90 91 92 93 94 95 / CH / 10 9 8 7 6 5 4 3 2

This book is lovingly dedicated to
John and Maggie Wiens

You have loved me as a daughter.
Thank you not only for sharing your lives
with me, but for sharing
your cherished culture and language.

Contents

■ ■ ■

III. COMMUNICATING WITH DEAF PEOPLE

Foreword

■ ■ ■

I HAVE ALWAYS been fascinated by language. I love French—it sounds so beautiful and graceful. I love Spanish, too—it is so elegant and expressive.

But most of all I love American Sign Language (ASL). It embodies the most graceful elements of the Romance languages and so much more.

The beauty of signing is one reason why I would learn ASL if I could use my hands. But there is another, more important reason.

There are more than 20 million hearing-impaired people in the United States alone. Within this group there exists a unique culture that has its own traditions, interests, and tastes, and—most important—its own language.

As Christians we have been called to communicate the gospel message to all people and cultures. This usually makes us think of missionary work somewhere in another country. In many ways that's a comforting thought, since few of us are called to active overseas ministry.

But our call is also to be missionaries to other cultures that exist in our own country. And we need the same level of discipline and commitment to reach these "next-door" cultures. If we are to minister effectively to deaf people, we must be willing to learn their language and customs and all that makes deaf culture interesting and unique.

That's why there is a special deaf ministry department of Joni and Friends. Unlike ministry to any other group of disabled people, deaf ministry is an outreach into a different culture. Effective ministry requires a willingness to learn a new language and to work hard to develop special skills. But it can be done, and the rewards of seeing communication barriers torn down can be wonderful indeed.

This tearing down of barriers and building of bridges with deaf people is what *A Guide to Deaf Ministry* is all about. This book contains all the key elements of what effective ministry to deaf people needs to do and be—from an understanding of deaf culture to an introduction to ASL.

I believe that *A Guide to Deaf Ministry* will broaden and deepen anyone's understanding of ministry to deaf people. It is a book not only for interpreters, but for families and friends of deaf people. It is for pastors, laypeople, sign-language students, those involved in existing deaf ministries, and those beginning a deaf ministry. In fact, *A Guide to Deaf Ministry* can serve as a valuable resource for hearing-impaired people who wish to help educate and encourage their hearing friends in the church.

Let me share one final word, however, to readers who are especially interested in sign language. This special book will not only increase your awareness of deaf culture and sharpen your signing skills, but also help you to handle effectively the responsibility of having the Word of God "on your hands." It is my prayer that God will use this book to help you and many other interpreters truly sign worthy of the Lord.

Joni Eareckson Tada
President, Joni and Friends
Chairman, Christian Council
      on Persons with Disabilities

Preface

■ ■ ■

O N A COLD winter's day in 1984, I was one of twenty thousand Christians attending a five-day missions conference in Urbana, Illinois. I had not come to the conference seeking a missionary opportunity for myself. God had been equipping me, calling me, and using me to share Christ with deaf people for many years. As I watched conferees review ministry options, I recalled how I had found mine.

From my very first sign-language class I had been enthralled with the language. I had wanted to communicate with my cousin, whose deafness was a by-product of the rubella epidemic of the sixties. But I was mesmerized by sign language and couldn't soak it in quickly enough. In the back of my mind I knew there was some larger purpose for my learning this fascinating language.

Upon my Christian conversion, I immediately desired to share Christ with deaf people. Involvement in deaf ministry soon became a significant part of my life. Whether pioneering a deaf ministry, working side by side with deaf people, or teaching a sign-language class, I wanted to be communicating God's love through this expressive, forthright language. I did so by teaching sign language and training interpreters at a community college, leading a deaf women's Bible study and deaf-ministry seminars around the nation.

The ultimate blessing came when I served as a short-term missionary in various parts of India. It was a thrill to see doors of communication opening up as I taught at deaf schools, introducing sign language to students and educators, both hearing and deaf. And I will never forget the time in Calcutta, India, when Mother Teresa flashed to me the sign "I love you." I thought to myself, "God's love truly is universal, regardless of the language barrier."

Why was I accompanying our church's college youth group to the InterVarsity missions conference in Urbana? The world needs God's love, and people are needed to share it. My husband and I had with us twenty-five students zealous to serve the Lord in whatever capacity God wanted. Among them were one deaf girl and two interpreters seeking deaf mission and ministry opportunities.

We listened to inspiring speakers, watched movie presentations, and collected literature detailing missionary opportunities throughout the world. Missions representatives were conducting on-the-spot interviews for those interested in specific cultures or locations. Yet, as we wandered among the maze of displays, there was little to nothing available for the deaf girl and interpreters whose hearts were eager to serve in a deaf ministry. For the first time I realized that a very vital culture in our own society was being overlooked.

Feelings of compassion mingled with frustration in me. I asked myself, "How will deaf people in this country 'hear' about Jesus Christ unless someone ministers to them in their own language? And how can that ministry take place unless those Christians called to serve deaf people are taught American Sign Language, educated about deaf culture, and trained to establish quality deaf ministries?" I sensed God's prodding in my heart as if there was something urgent I needed to do, but I didn't know what.

As the conference drew to a close, a representative of the United States Charter on World Missions presented some staggering statistics. There are 24,500 culture groups in the world, and of these, 17,500 have *never* heard the gospel. I asked myself, "Are the deaf people of this world considered among those 24,500? Are deaf people even considered a separate culture group to this speaker?"

As the missionary finished his speech and left the platform, I was at his side, asking these questions. He responded with love and enthusiasm for my concern toward deaf culture, but he had no concrete answers. Romans 10:17 seemed to pierce my heart: "Faith comes from hearing the message, and the message is heard through the word of Christ." I was determined somehow to reach the deaf culture that I knew exists throughout the world.

A quiet, gentle thought came to my mind. "You know, DeAnn, you ought to write a book."

I immediately objected, "Oh no, not *me!* What would I say?"

God replied by reminding me of his call to Moses (Ex. 4:10–13). Moses responded to God, "My Lord, I beg you to send another person. I'm not a good speaker and don't use the best words." I certainly had those feelings. I was definitely not an author and never dreamed of becoming one. However, God's call was clear; just as he provided a way for Moses to speak through Aaron, he provided me with the faith, stamina, and courage to tackle what seemed an impossible project and with a wonderful family and friends to stand beside me.

The proof of God's faithfulness is this book, *A Guide to Deaf Ministry.*

I do not consider myself to have "arrived" when it comes to writing, interpreting, ministering to deaf people, or even being a wife and a mother. In all these things I am "becoming." Likewise, this book is not an exhaustive, definitive resource on ministering with deaf people. My goal is to whet your appetite for American Sign Language, stimulate your awareness about deaf culture, inform you on the various methods of communication available to deaf people, and prepare you for more effective ministry to deaf people. Most of all I want to inspire you to keep "becoming" through the opportunities God has given you to serve a deaf brother or sister in Chirst.

Be aware that you *cannot* teach yourself sign language from a book. No matter how clear and precise the illustrations, they cannot convey the fine details of expression and context that make one fluent in sign language. By all means, obtain instruction at your nearest activities center or church. Seek out qualified instructors with a great deal of experience in sign language or those with deaf family members. Better yet, take a sign-language class from a deaf instructor. Then use the conversational phrases in this book as a springboard for conversing with deaf people in your church and community.

This book was created out of my desire that others begin communicating with the thousands of loving, stimulating deaf people who live in every neighborhood and community. To begin, *you* must put aside your own misconceptions and prejudices, break down the communication barrier, and cross into "their world." I hope the information shared in this book will equip you with many tools you need to communicate the love of Christ to deaf people. I pray God gives you the motivation and confidence to take the first step into a wonderful and exciting culture.

> *The LORD will fulfill his purpose for me;*
> *Your love, O LORD, endures forever—*
> *do not abandon the works of your hands.*
> **—PSALM 138:8**

Acknowledgments

■ ■ ■

NO PERSON'S WORK is hers alone, and this book—so long dreamed of—is now completed because of the prayers and support of many people. I want to thank each one and praise the Lord for—

Duane Anderson—The greatest illustrator around. Thanks for all the "strokes." Your creativity was an encouragement to the completion of this book.

Joel Burkum—Whose expertise created and produced the dynamic videotape that complements this book. A special thanks to your wife, *Pen,* who always keeps you organized.

Kristen Cloud—My precious friend and colleague, who gave hours of her time to model for illustrations in this book.

Sandra De Vera—Your brilliant touch on the computer will always be remembered.

Joni and Friends organization—

Joni—"Thank you" seems insignificant when I think of your belief in and support of this book, but thank you for loving deaf people too and for opening the door at Zondervan. I will be forever grateful.

Joe Davis—You led me step by step through that door. Your advice and encouragement are greatly appreciated.

Ross Arnold—You are not only the greatest editor, but a phenomenal organizer. Your serving and Christlike attitude has been a blessing to me.

Camille Beckham—Your being in "my corner" all along has been an inspiration to me. You are a fine example of a professional Christian interpreter.

In appreciation to all of you and your vision in this work as a valuable contribution to the field of deaf ministry, I say a big thank-you and I love you.

Duane King—President of Deaf Missions, who believed in, supported, and encouraged me in the projects God prompts me to do.

Samuel and Brenda Marsh—You have openly shared your lives and experiences so that others might minister more effectively. God bless you both for your obedience in leading deaf people to Christ. It has been an honor for me to serve side by side with such godly people.

The Bakersfield Christian deaf community—Thank you for loving me and accepting me into your culture and lives. These are *our* experiences, and this book is our contribution to advancing the message and the ministry of our Lord to many, many more deaf friends.

My family—

My husband—Michael, you believed in me and in this project through both the good and the hard times. Thank you for being my partner in ministry and joining me in the vision of *A Guide to Deaf Ministry* and for helping me to accomplish what God has called me to do. This book is "ours." I love you. (Genesis 2:18)

Nicole and Kristen—You always gave Mom time to work on "the book." Your patience and encouragement were an inspiration to me. Guess what, girls? It's all over! Let's go to K-Mart for some popcorn! (3 John 4)

My grandmother—(1899–1989). "Maw," don't worry, I will always strive for humility because of your admonition to keep things in perspective and not become one of those "educated fools." I miss you! (1 Thessalonians 4:16–17)

Finally, and most important, I would like to thank—

My Lord—Who considered me worthy to be called to such a task as this. May *you* be glorified on each and every page (1 Timothy 1:12)

... And there are others too numerous to list, whose roles are no less appreciated, but who themselves are unaware of how much they contributed.

I

UNDERSTANDING THE NEEDS OF DEAF PEOPLE

■ ■ ■

THE RIGHTS OF
THE DEAF CHILD

■ ■ ■

The right to be himself.
The right to know his own name.
The right to communicate with his
*   parents and receive love and under-*
standing from them.
The right to express himself in the
*   manner in which he feels most secure.*
The right to freedom from physical abuse.
The right to special care so that his
*   deafness does not become a handicap.*
The right to an appropriate education
*   for his individual needs.*
The right to make his own decisions.
The right to choose his own friends.
The right to reach his full potential
*   as a human being and not a weak*
*imitation of a "normal" child.**

ONE

What Is Deafness?

And as he went along, he saw a man blind [deaf] from birth. His disciples asked him, "Rabbi, who sinned, this man or his parents, that he was born blind [deaf]?" "Neither this man nor his parents sinned," said Jesus, "but this happened so that the work of God might be displayed in his life."

—JOHN 9:1–3

*I*N THE STORY of the man born blind, Jesus tells us that physical disabilities happen "in order that the works of God might be displayed." While his example concerned a blind man, the truth of his message is applicable to deaf people as well. In fact, we could replace the word *blind* with the word *deaf* to understand better why God has created deaf people.

Deafness is simply the inability to hear sound, with or without a hearing aid. Unfortunately, this definition obscures more than it clarifies. Deafness involves some problem in the auditory system. Its effects, however, spread far beyond the mere physical inability to receive sound effectively; it affects a person's entire life.

A hearing loss can have a devastating effect on one's ability to participate in society. Speech is our primary means of communication. When deafness strikes, it means that a person must develop an alternative method of communicating. If deafness occurs early in life, it threatens a child's ability to learn spoken language at all. Early deafness presents a staggering obstacle to mastering the structure of the English language, since this understanding usually comes from hearing the spoken language during childhood. Unless communication is quickly established in both the home and the educational setting, a child's ability to learn the language successfully will be greatly hindered.

There are many examples of the trauma that can occur in a family because of communication difficulties between hearing parents and their deaf child.

A friend of mine experienced frustration and disillusionment with the professionals around her who ignored her suspicions that her infant son was not responding as he should and might be deaf. Only after ricocheting from one doctor to another and repeatedly hearing those piercing words, "Oh, you're just overreacting," did she finally follow her motherly instincts. Setting aside her own denial, she had her son tested by an audiologist, who within three *minutes* confirmed that the boy was profoundly deaf in both ears. Then she felt compelled to reject the advice of a professional who said, "There is nothing you can do. Go home and love him and when he is four years of age, institutionalize him." This family proceeded not only to love and encourage their son, but also chose to be informed and educated regarding deafness and communication methods, which opened up a whole new world to them.

I read in the newspaper of another case in which the hearing mother of a deaf daughter stated, "When my daughter's hearing loss was first evaluated, the word *deaf* was never used. 'Hearing impaired' was the designation, carrying with it the idea of something broken, something that could be mended if only I worked hard enough."

Deafness is more widespread than most people realize. Almost everyone has a relative with a hearing impairment, whether a cousin who lost hearing at birth or a grandparent who has slowly lost hearing over the years. According to the National Information Center of Deafness in Washington, D.C.:

- 20,000,000 Americans are hearing impaired (1 in every 11 persons);
- As many as 2,000,000 people are deaf;
- 75,000 school-aged hearing-impaired children are receiving educational services;
- 25 percent of adults over the age of sixty-five have a hearing loss;
- 35 percent of adults over the age of seventy-nine have a hearing loss;
- 95 percent of deaf children have hearing parents.

Sooner or later, deafness touches all of us in some way. Among hearing-impaired people there is a great diversity of hearing loss, communication skills, and learning potential. It is important to deal with each hearing-impaired person according to the individual needs. Since the physiological aspects of a person's deafness helps determine his or her particular needs, it is extremely useful to have some understanding of the types and causes of deafness when ministering to deaf people.

When we say a person is "deaf," we might be speaking of anything from a mild loss of hearing to a severe loss. Edgar D. Lawrence states, "Just as we do not classify all people who wear glasses as blind, we cannot classify all who have a hearing loss as totally deaf."[1] There are many types and degrees of hearing loss that prevent us from clumping people into a single category, "deaf."

DEFINITIONS OF DEAFNESS

Most deaf people have some residual hearing that enables them to detect specific types of sound to varying degrees. They can react to certain sounds, but they do not hear them in the same way a person with normal hearing does. Hearing loss technically is classified according to the time the loss occurred and the amount of loss. Byron B. Burns, past president of the National Association of the Deaf, offers the following definitions:

A. *Deaf*—People in whom the sense of hearing is nonfunctional for the ordinary purposes of life. Input of sound is meaningless for communicational purposes. This general group is made up of two distinct classes based on the time of loss of hearing.

1. *Congenitally deaf:* Those who were born deaf.

2. *Adventitiously deaf:* Those who were born with normal hearing but in whom the sense of hearing became nonfunctional later in life through illness or accident. This is also called "acquired deafness."

There are two other classifications that refer to the onset of deafness.

3. *Prelingual deafness:* Deafness that was present at birth or occurred at an age prior to the development of speech and language.

4. *Postlingual deafness:* Deafness that occurs at an age following a spontaneous acquisition of speech and language.

B. *Hard of Hearing*—People in whom the sense of hearing, although defective, is functional with or without a hearing aid. They hear enough sound for it to have meaning. The term "hearing impaired" refers to *both* deaf and hard-of-hearing people.

TYPES OF HEARING LOSS

There are basically three types of hearing loss.

A. *Conductive deafness:* The term used to designate hearing losses resulting from deficiency of function in the outer or middle ear.

B. *Sensory-neural deafness:* The term used to designate hearing losses resulting from inner-ear deficiencies.

C. *Central deafness:* A condition in which the peripheral or receiving mechanism of hearing is functioning properly, but the person does not hear because of some injury or abnormality of the central nervous system.

You may wonder how important this technical information is for an effective ministry in the deaf community. It is important because in such a ministry we need to have a basic understanding of all aspects of deafness, its causes and effects. To deaf people, it is important what kind of hearing loss they have, their degree of loss, and when their loss occurred. These will probably be the topics of conversation early in your relationship with deaf people.

The major causes of hearing loss in America are—

■ Hereditary factors (Rh factor complications, Wardenburg syndrome)

- Complications during pregnancy (maternal rubella, premature birth)
- Childhood diseases (meningitis, encephalitis, measles, infection, high fever)
- Accidents
- Old age

Of the school-age population with known causes, maternal rubella was, until recently, the leading cause of deafness due to the 1964–65 epidemic. According to demographics, heredity and meningitis were the leading causes among deaf students in 1985.

Regardless of the cause of the disability, there is always a need for the deaf person to learn to communicate, to interact, and to express feelings. In the United States, deaf people use a variety of communication systems. Their choices include speaking, speech reading, writing, and manual communication.

METHODS OF COMMUNICATION

There are two primary methods of communication with and among deaf people. The first is manual communication, which is a generic term referring to the use of sign language and finger-spelling. The second is oral communication, which incorporates speech, residual hearing, and lip-reading.

Manual Communication

The three most common types of manual communication in addition to finger-spelling are American Sign Language, Signed Exact English, and Pidgin Signed English.

American Sign Language (ASL)

>   ASL is the native language of deaf adults and is a distinct language with structure and vocabulary different from English.

Signed Exact English (SEE)

>   SEE uses manual signs presented in the same order as spoken English.

Pidgin Signed English (PSE)

> PSE is not strictly ASL or SEE, but combines elements of both.

Finger-Spelling

> Used in all manual languages, finger-spelling is the use of handshapes representing each letter of the written alphabet.

The reason why multiple manual systems exist relates to differences in communication needs and different interpretations of the important communication and social needs of deaf people. ASL is the most visual and conceptual and therefore is more readily adapted to the social environment of the deaf community. SEE and PSE are more complex, but do teach a deaf child the structure of written English and may facilitate communication with the hearing world. SEE was devised primarily for use by parents and in educational settings.

Oral Communication

Deaf people—even those deaf from birth—can learn to speak and understand spoken English by reading lips. To develop clear speech, however, may require years of speech therapy. Lip-reading is very difficult because only about 30 percent of English sounds can be clearly understood from watching the lips. This means that effective oral communication may require a deaf person to be persistent, disciplined, and consistently trained for many years.

Because of the difficulty in learning oral communication, the danger of miscommunication, and the frustration that oral deaf people sometimes experience, they often supplement with manual communication in order to make for clearer, more accurate conversation.

BEYOND THE COMMUNICATION BARRIER

Many people today are challenging the communication barrier that stands between them and their deaf friends, colleagues, or neighbors. People who are willing to learn sign language are stepping into an unknown culture and leaving their comfort zone. This initial effort takes courage and discipline. It is not an easy task, but it can be rewarding if followed through with determination and perseverance.

Helen Keller, who was both blind and deaf, stated that blindness separates people from things, while deafness separates people from people. Deafness limits communication. This is important, not because people cannot hear sounds, but because they have difficulty fully participating in a world that depends on sound to get its ideas across.

The challenge is to establish communication that is meaningful. Because there are so many different types and degrees of hearing loss, with many different effects on a person's ability to communicate through sound, there is no single approach that meets the needs of everyone. Each deaf person is entitled to use the mode or combination that suits him or her best, whether it is through speech, sign language, finger-spelling, mime, or paper and pencil. We must always be aware that behind the hearing disability is a person with an unhandicapped mind and spirit, and we must try to find the approach or combination of approaches that can produce full, clear communication.

THEY SAY I'M DEAF

■ ■ ■

They say I'm deaf,
These folks who call me friend.
They do not comprehend.

They say I'm deaf,
And look on me as queer,
Because I cannot hear.

They say I'm deaf,
I, who hear all day
My throbbing heart at play
The song the sunset sings,
The joy of pretty things,
The smiles that greet my eye,
Two lovers passing by.

A brook, a tree, a bird:
Who says I have not heard?

Aye, tho' it must seem odd,
At night I oft hear God.
So many kinds I get
Of happy songs, and yet—
*They say I'm deaf!**

*Saul Kessler, *The Silent Muse* (Washington: Gallaudet University Alumni Association). Used by permission.

TWO

The Deaf Community

Therefore go and make disciples of all nations, baptizing them in the name of the Father and of the Son and of the Holy Spirit.

—MATTHEW 28:19

I MAGINE YOURSELF among hundreds of people at a bus depot. If asked to select from the crowd a blind person, a quadriplegic, and a deaf person, what would you look for? To detect someone who is visually impaired you might look for a white cane or a guide dog. Seeing a person in a wheelchair could help you identify someone with a physical disability. Now find someone who is deaf. But no one is wearing a shirt with D-E-A-F written across the front. There is someone with a hearing aid; he or she might be deaf. You see another person making gestures with his hands that vary in style and speed. Using sign language could indicate deafness or the presence of someone with impaired hearing. While these are all possible visual clues, they are not *absolute.* Many times you cannot detect physical signs of deafness until you try to communicate and experience difficulties in doing so.

Let's suppose that in our crowded bus depot, a hearing person and a deaf person meet and try to communicate. Typically, both of them will feel awkward, because the interaction is flawed and confused. The deaf person has difficulty understanding because he or she cannot hear. The hearing person has difficulty because the deaf person's speech may be unclear or absent.

Think back to how you felt the last time you could not make

yourself understood or could not understand what someone was determined to explain. The most common reaction is *frustration*. Because of the frustation inherent in awkward communication, the hearing society often becomes impatient with deaf people. Impeded communication may lead to misconceptions about the deaf person's intellectual capacity, and the hearing person becomes patronizing. The end result is frequently "mutual withdrawal."

Perhaps you have visited someplace where you didn't "speak the language." My Spanish vocabulary consists of *!hola!* (hi) and *gracias* (thanks). During a trip to Mexico I was often confused and frustrated. Repeatedly I was unable to share comments or questions because of the communication barrier that existed. I missed out on a great deal of information and excitement simply because I didn't speak the language.

During the trip I found myself comparing how I felt with how deaf people must feel every day. I became so frustrated that I even tried to use sign language to get my point across, but the local residents just looked at me as if I were crazy! I felt isolation and paranoia when my friends would converse semi-fluently with our taxi drivers or waiters and then break into laughter. I just knew they were talking about me!

The fact that my friends spoke Spanish created an immediate rapport and bond between them and the Hispanic people of that community. It was easier for the local citizens to communicate with my friends than with me.

In general, people take the easiest, most comfortable path in life, and deaf people are no different. They, too, find their social life more comfortable with other deaf people than with the hearing because of the ease of communication and the automatic bond that stems from using American Sign Language. It is more *difficult* for deaf people to have meaningful social relationships with hearing people unless both can communicate fluently in the same mode, whether it be oral communication, manual communication, or a combination of both.

More and more deaf people in the United States consider themselves part of a distinct cultural group. Those who accept this identity view themselves as belonging to a proud and distinctive culture group known as "the deaf community," comprising people who use ASL as their primary means of communication. Over the past century and a half, the deaf community has developed a rich social life and folklore. Through efforts to meet their special needs, deaf people have organized a nationwide and international network of social, religious, political, athletic, dramatic, scholastic, and literary organizations.

WHO BELONGS TO THE DEAF COMMUNITY?

The deaf community is similar to other culture groups in that it adheres to particular social norms and values which are passed down through people's lives. It is different from other culture groups in that one does not become a member through nationality. A person is not "born into" the deaf community. It is a unique community because members are drawn in and developed by other members. True membership comes only through an emotional identification.

There are many subgroups within the deaf community, including prelingual deaf, children of deaf parents, hard-of-hearing people, postlingual deaf, oral deaf, and at times hearing people who work with deaf people (such as teachers, interpreters, and deaf advocacy agency workers).

Membership in the deaf community depends on the following:

- A person's "attitude" toward deafness
- The decision to support the values and goals of the deaf community
- Acceptance or respect for ASL as the native *language* of the deaf community

These factors and a person's *adherence* to them are more important to a person's membership than whether or not a person is actually deaf. One could conceivably be deaf and choose not to identify himself or herself with the deaf community (fig. 2.1). Some people with hearing loss prefer to identify with and function as members of the "hearing world." Likewise, some hearing people are considered part of the deaf community because they actively support the values and goals of that community. Acceptance of a hearing person into the deaf community may take many years, however; past tensions between deaf and hearing cultures have prompted many deaf people to be suspicious of hearing people on first meeting. For that reason, hearing people may have to prove they are trustworthy before a relationship develops (fig. 2.1).

THE RELATIONSHIP OF ASL TO DEAF CULTURE

One thing principally defines and directs any culture: the language. This is especially true with deaf culture, since it is American Sign Language that makes the distinct culture possible. ASL is the dominant language among deaf people in the United States, and their use of it must be understood in order to understand deaf culture.

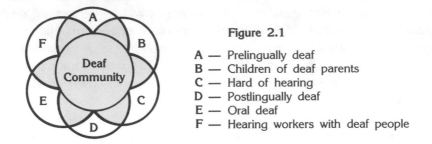

Figure 2.1

A — Prelingually deaf
B — Children of deaf parents
C — Hard of hearing
D — Postlingually deaf
E — Oral deaf
F — Hearing workers with deaf people

Ninety-five percent of hearing-impaired children in the United States are born into hearing families who have no prior knowledge of deafness. As these children mature and try to communicate their thoughts and feelings to their hearing parents, misunderstandings are almost inevitable. Even parents who make the effort to learn sign language will seldom have as much fluency in manual communication as a child who is deaf from birth. The result is confusion and poor communication, leading to conflict and frustration for everyone, especially the deaf child.

Deaf children growing up in hearing families have difficulty participating in any family discussion, such as talk around the dinner table. As a result, the children miss a sense of belonging and lack the opportunity to learn family and social values that are commonly communicated at mealtimes and in other family gatherings.

Research has shown that deaf children with deaf parents have a much different childhood environment. They have the benefit of years of mealtime discussions in ASL and, as a result, their social values and language development remain appropriate to their age level.

As human beings we need to communicate. We need to express emotion. We need feedback. When these needs are not met at home (as is often the case for a deaf child with hearing parents), children often look to school relationships for personal and social information.

The residential school environment is one common experience shared by the majority of deaf children in America. Deaf children who attend deaf schools eat, sleep, study, and play together apart from hearing students their own age. Most stay on campus through the week and return to their families on the weekend. The residential school becomes their "home away from home" and is often their first introduction to the deaf community and ASL. The deaf child feels, "At last! I can communicate. I can understand and be understood. These children are like me. What freedom!"

But with the blessing of newfound acceptance in a community there comes another hurdle—the problem of English versus ASL. English is usually taught in deaf school classrooms. Even when teachers sign, they often use Signed Exact English. Deaf children who grow up with ASL may have a difficult time understanding teachers who use SEE; ASL is visual and conceptual, while English has a very formal structure and word order.

Both hearing and deaf people become confused when comparing ASL and English, and serious problems occur when trying to integrate the two in an educational setting. Such struggles have caused some educators to challenge the use of ASL. Authorities in the past have doubted whether ASL can be considered a "language," claiming instead that it is a set of gestures which can communicate only the most basic messages.

One deaf girl recalls, "The teachers read my writing and complained that it was confused and out of order, blaming it on ASL, my 'wrong' language. They didn't understand or respect my language or my background. It was frustrating for me. Because I didn't know any better, I agreed with my teachers and blamed my struggles with English on ASL."

Linguistic research in recent years has shown that ASL is more than just a simple set of gestures and mime. The predominant conclusion has been that American Sign Language is indeed a full-fledged and viable language. This is an important issue to deaf people because deaf culture is founded on the premise that ASL is a complete language.

There is some new thinking among educators that ASL could be used to *enhance* English development in the classroom. This opinion is based on experience with public school bilingual programs. A Hispanic child with no English background would be given information in his native tongue and from that point would be introduced to a second language—English.

Educators feel this mode of instruction could easily be used with deaf children—that is, feeding them knowledge through ASL, then teaching them English as a second language.

It is the belief of many in the deaf community that, yes, English should be taught in school, but not to replace or exclude ASL.

LEVELS WITHIN THE DEAF COMMUNITY

There are several levels or layers of involvement in the deaf community, based on the extent to which members accept the language, values, and experiences of that culture (fig. 2.2). At the core of the deaf community are people who accept, defend, and use ASL as their primary form of communication. They are primarily prelingual deaf people who learned to use ASL prior to any use of English. They are the "gatekeepers" of the community and preserve and pass on the values of the culture.

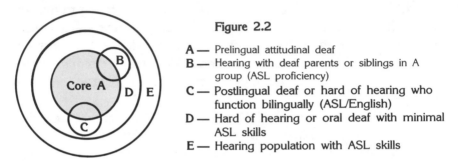

Figure 2.2

A — Prelingual attitudinal deaf
B — Hearing with deaf parents or siblings in A group (ASL proficiency)
C — Postlingual deaf or hard of hearing who function bilingually (ASL/English)
D — Hard of hearing or oral deaf with minimal ASL skills
E — Hearing population with ASL skills

Hearing children of deaf parents often find themselves in the core of the deaf community as well. As adults some may choose to remain in the deaf culture, serving as interpreters to their enlarged "family." Others will leave the deaf community and make hearing society their primary choice.

Other people who might find themselves in the core of the deaf community are postlingual deaf and hard-of-hearing people who function bilingually (ASL/English). They also choose the deaf community as their primary "home" and are most comfortable with ASL even though English remains an option for them.

At the second level in the deaf community are hard-of-hearing and oral deaf people who have minimal ASL skills. They are closer to the core than their hearing friends with ASL skills because of physiological similarities, but until they fully value the goals of deaf culture they are not likely to be immersed in the deaf community.

As with all models, there are exceptions. I have known hearing people with no deaf relatives who functioned at the core of the deaf community and should be considered "core members." These people often prefer the deaf culture to the hearing culture and spend the majority of their time with the deaf community.

Figure 2.3

Language	Experiences	Activities
American Sign Language (ASL)	Rejection Paranoia Misunderstanding Frustration Interpreters/writing notes Isolation/seclusion Legal difficulties Economic frustrations Communication problems Limited education Attitude barriers Mainstreaming programs Job discrimination Residential schools Speech therapy Hearing aids Audiograms Telecommunication Device for the Deaf (TDD) Supplementary Salary Income (SSI) Vocational Rehabilitation (VR) Closed captioned movies (CC) Community, family, church, and societal barriers	Deaf club Regional tournaments Political associations Deaf advocacy agencies Community centers Deaf schools World Games for the Deaf (Deaf Olympics) School reunions Newsletters National Theatre for the Deaf (NTD) National Association for the Deaf (NAD) Special tours Churches

BINDING FACTORS OF THE DEAF COMMUNITY

People in the deaf community may be found anywhere. They may live in large cities or rural farming communities. They may work as lawyers or custodians. Their reading ability may be at the third grade level or the graduate school level. Regardless of their differences, deaf people share many common experiences that bind them together and form their culture.

There are three basic components that shape deaf culture and give it cohesiveness: language, experience, and activities. We have already discussed ASL—its native language. Figure 2.3 is a list of experiences and activities that are shared in the community.

These activities are important in the deaf community because people are usually scattered over a wide area. Deaf people are somewhat isolated, so they depend on these activities for the majority of their socialization. They love to get together for information exchange and for a chance to use pure ASL. They depend on monthly club meetings, worship services, and social gatherings to catch up on the latest happenings within the community. Deaf functions usually feature much unity, lots of hugs, and hands gesturing continually. Occasionally the lights will blink on and off to get people's attention. It is amazing how fast "news" travels via the hands of the deaf community.

HISTORY OF DEAF EDUCATION

It is astonishing to consider that "normal" hearing education is thousands of years old, while formal education for the deaf has existed for a little more than two hundred years. Pioneered in France, deaf education was introduced in the United States in 1817 through the work of Thomas Gallaudet. The approach was based on sign language, and it seemed to produce a high rate of literacy among deaf people. One historian estimates that by 1869, 41 percent of the teachers of deaf people were themselves deaf.[1] Despite an undercurrent of dissent from some educators regarding the signing approach, deaf education was flourishing and bearing good fruit.

A turning point came in the 1870s, when the opponents of signing gained preeminence. The advocates of this approach viewed the goal of deaf education as the task of teaching deaf people to speak. Sign language was denigrated and discouraged; English became the language of instruction. The result was that by the turn of the century, illiteracy among deaf people had mushroomed, few deaf teachers remained, and the highly successful work of the past hundred years had been largely undone. (There was one exception. Oliver Sacks writes, "There has been one realm where sign language always continued to be used, all over the world, despite the changed habits and proscriptions of educators—in religious services for the deaf. Priests and others never forgot the souls of their deaf parishioners, learned Sign, ... and conducted services in Sign, right through the endless wrangles over oralism and the eclipse of Sign in secular education.")[2]

This was the sorry state of affairs until a turn away from "oralism" and a resurgence of sign language began to take hold in the 1960s, culminating in the protests at Gallaudet University in Washington, D.C., in March 1988.[3] At Gallaudet, the desire of deaf people to regain control over their education was demonstrated as the students campaigned against the faculty and board of directors for a "Deaf President Now." The worldwide attention brought by the protests helped the students achieve their goal.

What struggles have deaf people had to overcome to reach this new era of "deaf power" and "deaf pride"? Lack of employment has been and still is one of the most serious problems for deaf people. Deaf people want to enter the job market, but potential employers often believe that something other than deafness must be wrong with deaf applicants, and they assume that deaf people cannot do even those jobs that do not require hearing.

Even after being hired, deaf people face many problems. They are often held at entry-level positions far below their hearing peers because of discrimination. Whether intentional or not, employers may neglect deaf people primarily because the deafness is not visible. While great strides are being made to accommodate people with other disabilities— such as laws to require wheelchair ramps—most employers still ignore the needs of the deaf.

Without legislation that specifically addresses their needs, deaf people often go unnoticed unless *they* themselves confront the communication barrier. Such confrontation often produces further frustration among both hearing and deaf people because of the communication problems. Consequently, many deaf people become discouraged. They *expect* rejection and discrimination, so they feel intimidated or inferior. In desperation they may accept jobs below their true ability.

Some deaf people do fight for employment rights and become politicians, doctors, pastors, lawyers, actors, and other professionals. The potential is certainly present in deaf people, but the current employment environment leaves far too many of them sitting at home, unemployed, and dependent on government support.

Yet the changing approach to deaf education is ushering in a new era in deaf culture. We may begin to see more deaf people in the limelight and in leadership positions; we can expect that more hearing people will become educated in sign language and deaf culture. The hearing and deaf cultures may blend as one. As I. King Jordan, the new president of Gallaudet University, has said, "Deaf people can do anything hearing people can do . . . except hear."

OPENING DOORS THROUGH MODERN TECHNOLOGY

Modern technology and computers have created many new communication opportunities for deaf people. A Telecommunication Device for the Deaf (TDD) attaches to the telephone and allows a deaf person to type a message to another person with a similar device. A TDD can be purchased for as little as $150. In some states, deaf people receive a free TDD upon verification of deafness from an audiologist (see chapter 9 for information).

Television and film access for the deaf population is increasing. Telecaption decoders (or adaptors), either built into or attached to a television set, enable deaf viewers to read program dialogue on the TV screen. The signal is carried invisibly, so captions are seen only when the decoder is in operation. For the first time in network programming, the entire prime-time schedules of the three major networks are entirely closed captioned. This recent increase in captioned programming is making the investment of about two hundred dollars for a TV decoder much more attractive than before.

Modern technology has also made possible the development of many devices to assist hearing-impaired people:

Phone amplifiers	Wake-up timers that vibrate the bed
Burglar alarms	Hearing aids
Baby criers	Hearing implants
Doorbell signalers	Visual Alert Systems: special alarm
Smoke and fire alarms	systems for hotels and motels that
Answering machines	alert hearing-impaired or deaf people
Pagers	to a smoke alarm, a knock at the
Phone signalers	door, or a ringing telephone

Through the perseverance of the deaf community, public services such as hospitals, fire departments, and law-enforcement agencies have installed TDD devices so that deaf people can communicate in emergencies. Deaf advocacy services have been established to provide numerous services:

Interpreter referral service	Community education workshops
Information and referral service	Written materials (books on deafness)
Social security advocacy	Telephone relay service (whereby a deaf
Independent living skills	person can call a hearing operator with
Peer counseling	a TDD and communicate to a hearing
Job placement	person who does not have a TDD)
Sign language classes	

Many public agencies are working to improve social, educational, economic, and cultural conditions for the deaf and hard-of-hearing communities. These services have dramatically improved the quality of life for these people and their families. But what is the church doing? Are the *spiritual* needs of deaf people being met?

THE SPIRITUAL NEEDS OF DEAF PEOPLE

Duane King, the founder and president of Deaf Missions, writes in "Serving With Persons Who Are Deaf":

What is the worst "handicap"? The worst handicap is not to be deaf, or blind, or emotionally crippled, or confined to a wheelchair, nor even to have all of these handicaps at once. The worst handicap of all is to meet God on Judgment Day without Jesus as Savior. This is a handicap which cannot be overcome, and which is eternally devastating.

Once we have an understanding of the facts and figures, the controversy over communication methods and high-tech implants, the issue of public agency effectiveness, what are we left with? People. Ordinary people comprising body, mind, and spirit. Behind the labels "hearing impaired" and "physically challenged" are individuals with hopes and dreams, opinions and interests—some of whom may have never "heard" the saving message of Jesus Christ.

George B. Joslin challenges the churches to meet the needs of all people. He states:

Deaf people are Anglo and Latin American, Caucasian, Black and Oriental; adults and children, smart and ignorant; rich, middle class, and poor; good and bad; well educated and illiterate. They include children who know the language of signs and those who are being educated orally. Each of them challenges our churches to minister to his/her special need.

Is the church deliberately discriminating against deaf people? I think not. But how can the church environment become more conducive to providing spiritual growth for deaf children and hearing-impaired people in general?

A frustrated mother relates,

My son ought to have the same opportunity that hearing children do. Must his deafness exclude my son from the opportu-

nity to be taught God's Word? He is ten years old, and we have already waited too long! So many times we have brought our son to Vacation Bible School and there's nothing for him. How many times have we gone to a Bible conference and again met the same void. How many times must we attend Christian camps, only to be met with smiling faces. It's not that Christians don't care. They are just unable to communicate, or lack the knowledge that there is even a need. Through the years we have been our son's ears. Now I am tired and burned out, yet my son is hungry and thirsty for more. We feel alone.

God's Word declares that we all are born with the desire to know God (Rom. 1:19). Deafness does not affect the innate void in all of us that only God can fill. Deaf people are no different from any other culture group. They too need to "hear" the good news of Jesus Christ and his love. May our prayer always be:

Lord, as I attempt to share you and your love with those who may have never heard the gospel, please help me to be sensitive to them. May I never disrespect their language, try to manipulate their culture, or present myself as superior in any way. Help me to represent you and only you, as I leave my world to enter theirs. Amen.

II

CALLING THE CHURCH TO CHURCH TO DEAF MINISTRY

■ ■ ■

BEGIN WITH A HANDSHAKE
GIVE ME A SIGN

Sometimes I wonder,
How does it sound
When red leaves in autumn
Drift to the ground?
Can the pond's ripple
Speak to the tree?
Want to share your world?
Please share your world,
Please share mine with me.
Sometimes I'm lonely,
Want to reach out to you.
But silence between us
Is hard to break through.
So when I smile at you,
Hold out your hand.
Please know that your handshake
*Means you understand.**

*By Mary Jane Rhodes. Used by permission.

THREE

Where Do I Begin?

*But you, be sober in all things, endure hardships,
do the work of an evangelist, fulfill your ministry.*

—2 TIMOTHY 4:5 NASB

*A*NY WORTHWHILE MINISTRY begins within a pure heart. We start with our own relationship with Christ and then obey the Great Commission related in Matthew 28:19:

> Therefore go and make disciples of all nations, baptizing them in the name of the Father and of the Son and of the Holy Spirit.

"All nations" refers to all people, regardless of sex, race, culture, or whether they are deaf, hearing, able bodied, or disabled. We are commissioned to go!

Before becoming involved in deaf work, I was burdened with the following questions:

- If deaf people can't hear physically, how will they "hear" about Jesus Christ and his message of salvation?
- Who will share with them God's plan of hope, just as my physical education instructor did with me years ago?

I wrestled with these questions in my mind until I found comfort in Romans 10:13–15. As I studied these verses, certain words and concepts seemed to jump out at me.

For, "*Everyone* [deaf or hearing] who calls on the name of the Lord will be saved." How, then, can *they* [including deaf people] call on the one they have not believed in? And how can *they* believe in the one of whom *they have not heard?* And how can *they* hear without someone preaching to them? And how can *they* preach unless *they* are sent? As it is written, "How beautiful are the feet [and hands] of those who bring good news!"

When I was a new Christian, my heart was open and full of desire to share the message of Jesus Christ and the joy that comes from having a personal relationship with him. I remember bubbling over with enthusiasm as I told my friend Emarie that I had asked God to use me in deaf ministry and that I had given him my hands to use in any way he desired. Emarie was discipling me at the time, and her response was both encouraging and candid. "Remember," she said, "when you ask to be used of God, you'd better mean it! He can do great and mighty things through a genuine sacrifice of service."

My heart was like a child's, full of innocence and zeal, ready and willing for God to use me. Three years later, I was visiting deaf schools in India and traveling around the United States sharing God's message with deaf people through sign language.

Quite honestly, I had very little knowledge of deaf ministries and the appropriate methods needed to establish them. I shudder at the memory of some situations I found myself in as a beginning interpreter. But even though I sometimes felt inadequate and unworthy, I trusted God. He had given me skill to communicate through sign language. He had made and placed deaf people on this earth, and he desired to have an eternal relationship with them. Despite my limitations, God looked on a servant's willing heart and created fruitful works.

I challenge you to examine your motives if you are considering any aspect of deaf ministry. I have seen people begin ministries—or even relationships—with deaf people but soon lose interest. Perhaps they were first motivated by the novelty of using ASL and didn't know the needs of those they were seeking to serve. Maybe they began their "work" for selfish reasons, since a lot of praise and attention is often given to a "new" deaf ministry leader. As with any ministry, the encouragement fades after a while, and the emotional strokes diminish.

A servant's heart is required for working with deaf people. The needs of those served are more important than the servant's need for approval and praise. The hopes of many deaf people have been shattered time and again by a new sign language student who wants to interpret for them, have a Bible study with them, or establish a friendship—only to lose commitment or interest later on. Please, before making a commitment to a deaf friend, make certain your motive is one that God will honor.

I must strive to examine my motives daily and compare them with those of our Lord Jesus as expressed in Philippians 2. Jesus humbled himself and became obedient to the point of death on a cross. He could have become selfish and insisted on having his own needs and desires met, but he set them aside, made the sacrifice, and committed himself to serving us. He gave us the hope of eternal life. We have the privilege of sharing this hope and following the example of his obedience and service with humility. We need to pray:

> Lord, make me like you. Help me see my heart as you see it. Oh, that I might be a humble, obedient, and genuine servant as I serve those I am called to serve.

WHO, ME—A MISSIONARY?

I have read numerous stories about how overseas missionaries train to present God's message to a different culture. They study for years to learn the language they will need in their mission.

When hearing people enter the deaf culture for the purpose of ministry, they are missionaries. As missionaries they need to take seriously the responsibility of preparing well for service. The first step is to learn the language of deaf people—American Sign Language.

Learning some basic sign language phrases as found in this book will allow you to start communicating with deaf people at a personal level in your church and community. From there, if God calls you to a deeper ministry with deaf people, you can get additional training. But learning your first signs is only a beginning. If you work hard and master American Sign Language, you will reap a bountiful harvest in your friendships and service with deaf people.

LEARNING AND RESPECTING THE LANGUAGE

Once we have developed the skill of sign language and have a deep desire to involve ourselves in deaf work, we must strive to work *alongside* deaf people, not *for* "the poor deaf people." One of our goals in deaf ministry should be to develop deaf leaders. Deaf people should be leading deaf people whenever possible. That does not mean there is no room for the hearing person in a deaf church or deaf ministry. There are many important roles for skilled and committed hearing people. Still, there is a need for more deaf pastors, for more obedient and godly men and women to open their hearts and heed the call of deaf work. No one can meet the needs of deaf people better than the deaf themselves.

I will never forget the impact a deaf pastor's message had on me. The deaf members of my church had recently chosen to meet separately and conduct their own worship services. The deaf ushers had seated the people, handed out programs, and collected the offering. A deaf woman led the worship choruses and announced upcoming events. It was time for the guest speaker to begin his sermon. All congregational signing came to a halt. Eyes were intently fixed on the deaf pastor. The silence was intense. There was eager anticipation on each and every deaf person's face in that congregation. Each was ready to catch every biblical truth about to be presented in their own tongue.

Just before the guest pastor began his sermon, he signed, "True, wonderful worship God own language" (Isn't it wonderful to worship God in our own language?).

That statement hit me hard, and a tear trickled down my cheek as I thought, "Well, of course, don't Hispanics, Chinese, and African people want to hear the gospel in their own language? Don't junior high and high school groups like to meet with their peers? Don't I enjoy—even *need*—hearing sermons in my native language? It is the language I feel confident with, a language I can relax with, a language by which I can receive most of my knowledge and information."

That is what I saw happening among the deaf congregation that memorable day. They, too, wanted to be free to worship and fellowship and be taught in the way that was most natural and comfortable to them—their own language.

EDUCATING THE CHURCH BODY

Once we have the burden, the vision, the love, and the means to communicate effectively, the next preparatory stage takes place within the body of Christ, the church. Before we extend the invitation for deaf people to come and worship with us, we will want to be sure that our congregation is ready to receive them with confidence and love.

Millions of deaf people around the world have been overlooked by the church. I once heard a colleague state that deaf people are the "forgotten" people. This is true, not because our society intentionally neglects them or is indifferent toward them; rather, the deaf community are an *unknown* people to the majority of the people in the church.

Government agencies, schools, colleges, civic clubs, and associations are pouring millions of dollars into assisting and accommodating deaf people. But as necessary and helpful as this is, it is temporal. The church as a whole lags far behind in providing for the spiritual and social needs of its deaf members. Many deaf people have had only superficial exposure to Christianity, consisting mainly of Sunday school classes in a residential school. Often these classes are taught by people having little or no religious preference, much less having a personal faith commitment to Jesus Christ. We can only be thankful for those teachers who do teach the fundamentals of the Christian faith at the residential schools, and we can pray that their number will increase.

If the situation in our churches is to improve, we must accept responsibility to lovingly educate our congregations about the special needs of the deaf people they may once have shunned. If you have the skills and commitment for deaf ministry, I encourage you, with help from a deaf friend or church member, to begin educating your church. You might start by teaching a basic ASL class or inviting a professional to teach a class. Whatever it takes, help *inform* and *educate* the people on deaf culture and communication. Strive to eliminate any prejudices and misunderstandings. Break down those barriers.

THROWING MISCONCEPTIONS OUT THE WINDOW

Many hearing people have misconceptions about deaf people. For example, they tend to think that a person who wears a hearing aid must be able to hear human speech to a little degree. In fact, most hearing aids only assist a deaf person in reading lips. Another misconception is that a deaf person with good eyesight can be expected to read well. But people who have been deaf from birth or an early age have only an elementary understanding of written English; in effect, English is a second language.

I once heard a blind woman say that "apathy" is the social handicap of our society. According to the Standard College Dictionary, *apathy* means "a lack of interest or emotion, an unconcern which suggests lack of an appropriate response or an unwillingness to become personally involved." Apathy arises from a kind of selfishness that can affect any of us. It is human nature for us not to want to put ourselves out for others or be inconvenienced. This tendency can affect our attitudes not only toward people with disabilities but also our families, Bible study, our neighbors, our jobs, and our churches.

But apathy is not rooted entirely in selfishness. It may also come from *nescience,* a word that means "a lack or absence of knowledge; ignorance." We need to understand that apathy may be just a *temporary* lack of interest caused by ignorance rather than mere callousness or absorption in our own affairs. If the problem is a lack of understanding or knowledge, that can change. But we alone can perceive the true intentions of our hearts.

Regardless of our reasons, most people feel reluctant to approach a person who is in a wheelchair or has to rely primarily on hands for communication. Yet it is only a lack of knowledge and experience that prevents us from feeling comfortable and confident enough to reach out in genuine love.

As we gain knowlege and insight into deafness, sign language, and deaf culture, we will hopefully begin to develop interest, concern, and sensitivity and have the willingness to become personally involved in the lives of deaf people. Remember, knowledge plus insight minus misconceptions equals love.

If we accept the challenge to educate people, to help them overcome their reluctance to relate to deaf people, we should strive to do so in the most effective way possible. Be creative!

One approach might be to ask members of the congregation to share their fears and questions. Discuss with them the following misconceptions and "dos and don'ts."

Misconceptions

It must be emphasized that deaf people are not—

Mentally retarded. Deaf people have normal intellects. Some may, however, lag behind their hearing colleagues in academic achievement because of the language barrier and/or inadequate education.

Unfriendly. People with hearing impairments tend to congregate with other hearing-impaired persons and may therefore appear to be unfriendly. If *you* initiate conversation and demonstrate a genuine interest, you will find deaf people to be friendly and patient.

Bad drivers. Some people assume that deaf people, because they are unable to hear traffic sounds, must be bad drivers. It has been proven that deaf drivers are very competent as long as they don't try to talk with their hands while driving! In general, deaf drivers are more visually alert than hearing drivers and can concentrate better, undistracted by a radio or noisy children.

WHAT TO DO AND NOT DO
IN RELATING TO DEAF PEOPLE

- **Do not** use the phrases "deaf mute" or "deaf and dumb." The correct terms are "deaf," "hard of hearing," or "hearing impaired." **Do** ask the deaf person which he prefers. Remember, this is the era of Deaf Pride.
- **Do not** talk fast, mumble, or shout. It doesn't help. **Do** carry a small pad and pencil in case communication becomes frustrating, or for writing down pertinent information.
- **Do not** cover your face with your hands or objects. **Do** maintain eye contact with the deaf person you are talking to. Let his eyes and face speak to you and let your face be expressive. Throw your inhibitions out the window and let your face and body do the talking.
- **Do not** allow others to interrupt when you are conversing with a deaf person. This is common etiquette that people tend to forget. If you talk with a deaf person with the help of an interpreter, **do** talk to the deaf person directly; **do not** talk toward the interpreter. Avoid saying to the interpreter, "Tell the deaf person . . ." (This is a good exercise for role playing.)
- **Do not** pretend to understand when you don't. Swallow your pride and shake your head "no." Ask the deaf person to repeat the statement or to write it down. Otherwise, you may find yourself in an embarrassing situation.
- **Do not** ignore a deaf person who is present in a group of hearing people. **Do** include the deaf person as much as possible in the conversation.
- **Do not** correct a deaf person's English (unless he asks for help).
- **Do not** let fear of making mistakes in your sign language keep you from approaching a deaf person. If you can't sign, face the deaf person directly and speak slowly, but not in an exaggerated fashion. (It is helpful if beards and mustaches are well trimmed.)

- **Do not** use puns or idioms unless you know the deaf person has a good command of the English language. But **do** include deaf people when telling jokes; otherwise, they may think you're laughing at them. Be sensitive.
- **Do not** single out a person because you find their deafness a novelty. Treat a deaf person as you would a hearing person. Share the attitudes, desires, and interests you have in common. Choose a deaf person for a friend because of commonalities, not because of the disability.
- Never throw paper or another object to get a deaf person's attention. Tap him on the shoulder or wave your hand. In large groups you may flick the lights on and off.

Be sure to involve the deaf people in all the aspects of church life such as skits, Sunday school lessons, special events, and social gatherings. Allow deaf people to usher or serve Communion—even lead in prayer along with an interpreter. Every bit of exposure the deaf members receive will in turn educate the church body. Remember, deaf people need what all people need—a sense that they are respected as whole persons, leaders, communicators. What better place to receive this sense of self-esteem than in the church!

DEAF COMMUNITY, HERE I COME

In speaking of the church's role in serving the deaf community, we must accept the reality that not every congregation will be able to have a deaf ministry. However, the church can learn to think of deaf people as a unique culture with special needs. If our church does want to establish a deaf work, the first step is to assess the size and needs of the deaf community around us. You can be certain that there *is* a deaf cluster in the area, whether large or small.

To locate the deaf people in the community, begin this way:

- Check local listings for deaf advocacy agencies.
- Check the local post office, social security office, or vocational rehabilitation center for the number of deaf people in the community. (These institutions cannot give out names and addresses.)
- Check the local newspapers (1) for churches with established deaf ministries or interpreted services, and (2) for regularly

scheduled social events. Invite yourself and attend one of these functions with a deaf friend.

- Check local colleges and adult schools that may have a deaf program and sign language courses.
- Walk the neighborhood and, even though you might feel odd doing so, ask neighbors if they have deaf family or friends in the community. I tried this and discovered that a deaf boy was living only three blocks from my home.

If our congregation is serious about establishing a deaf ministry, a probe study is essential in determining what type of ministry is needed. There is no better way to get accurate and precise answers than going straight to the source. Use the deaf approach and ask deaf people you meet directly—they will appreciate your method:

- Are you interested in attending church?
- What are you looking for in a church?
- Would you attend a Bible study if the group is small?
- Would you like to study the Bible one on one?
- Would you be interested in a potluck supper followed by a short devotional talk or a videotaped Bible story?

The list could go on, but the point is to assess individual needs. We cannot start a total deaf program with the vague idea that "we should have one." But we may be able to meet the needs of one individual.

Ideally, as the deaf ministry expands, we will develop a core of deaf leaders who will be prepared to make important decisions regarding the direction of the church's ministry. Some possibilities:

- Integration of deaf members into the hearing church with a sign language interpreter and/or a mainstreamed deaf-and-hearing Sunday school class with interpreting provided. (Technically speaking, this is an "interpreting service" and *not* a deaf ministry.)
- A separate Sunday school class led by a deaf teacher
- A separate midweek Bible study, using videotape visuals and taught by a deaf teacher
- A separate deaf worship service, using deaf leadership and receiving support from the hearing congregation
- An indigenous, self-supporting, all-deaf church with a deaf pastor

Keep in mind that the goal for any church, whether for deaf or hearing, is that the gospel of Jesus Christ go forth clearly and distinctly. I pray that the church's relationship to the deaf community will be, first of all, one of "openness." Our awkwardness toward communication can be eliminated by learning a few sentences of welcome and encouragement found in this book. The barrier of our ignorance can be replaced by taking the time to educate ourselves about a new culture and a new language. And most important, we can seek to remove any obstacles that hinder the natural flow of God's love.

HEEDING THE CALL

How do we know if we are *called* to deaf ministry? Does proficiency in the language of signs or does being a child of deaf parents make one a natural candidate?

Proficiency and academic training alone do not qualify us for ministry, nor does being the child of deaf parents. Rather, it is the love and conviction in our hearts and minds that God truly desires for us to minister to a special segment of humanity. In his powerful book *Real Christians Don't Dance!* John Fischer states:

> There is no magic to ministry. No aura. No privilege. Ministry is simply service. Jesus Christ set the supreme example by divesting himself of all privileges as God and humbly taking on the form of a servant. He himself declared, "For even the Son of Man did not come to be served, but to serve, and to give his life as a ransom for many" (Mark 10:45). Ministry is what you give, not what you get. And probably, the most important of all—there is no primacy to ministry. Nothing sets one Christian over another. There should be no sense of superiority in any ministry, because the Scriptures clearly teach that all of us are ministers. Each of us is responsible for serving according to the *gifts* that have been given to us. No single ministry is more important than another.[1]

You may be saying to yourself, "Those are powerful words, and in my heart I do want to serve, but I don't know what my gifts are. How can I discern my spiritual gifts?" According to Scripture, each of us does have a spiritual gift or gifts, and it is important that we discover what they are. Ministries are based on spiritual gifts. Spiritual gifts need to be discerned in the context of the church, and there must be specific training in the exercise of these gifts.

We can take encouragement from 1 Corinthians 12:4–6, which says:

> There are different kinds of gifts, but the same Spirit. There are different kinds of service, but the same Lord. There are different kinds of working, but the same God works all of them in all men.

Taking the "Discerning Your Spiritual Gifts" questionnaire (found at the end of this chapter) may help you to recognize the type of ministry God has equipped you for or even identify gifts you have never recognized.

Along with discerning our spiritual gifts we must strive to develop our natural talents as in music, art, or sign language. Not all people can develop the art of sign language with proficiency. Some people seem to have a natural, God-given ability to coordinate signs with grace and fluency and to have the hand-eye coordination and mental ability it requires to retain the new language. Others just find it too difficult to absorb the basics of communication and knowledge regarding deaf people and their language.

So as we begin the preparatory process for deaf ministry, we should ask ourselves:

- Does sign language come easily to me?
- Do I perceive signs correctly and desire to use my signs with deaf people?
- Do I have a natural ability to make the message of God visual, so deaf people can understand his message of salvation in their own language (i.e., changing abstract concepts into easy-to-grasp visual concepts)?
- Do I truly enjoy deaf people and feel comfortable in the deaf community?
- Do deaf people seek my company?
- If I am married, do my spouse and children enjoy interacting with deaf people? (This question demands a unanimous response.)

MINISTRY WITHIN OUR SPHERE OF INFLUENCE

Just as every believer is called to ministry and is spiritually gifted and empowered for service, each one also has a unique sphere of influence. Let's go beyond the four walls of the church and into the unique and challenging culture of the deaf community.

If we have determined that God has called us to deaf work, we must make the deaf community our sphere of influence. Our sphere of influence is the relationships we have cultivated through our home, neighborhood, church, leisure activities, job, and relatives. Are deaf people included in any of these clusters?

Keep in mind that the size of our circle is not so important as the faithfulness to minister within it. Looking at the apostle Peter as an example, we see that his sphere of influence was much larger than his brother Andrew's—yet it was Andrew who led Peter and several others to Christ. Also, the Bible portrays Lydia as quite the "socialite" with a broad sphere of influence, in contrast with the Samaritan woman whom Jesus met at the well. Yet each had a significant impact on her circle of associates. Thinking in terms of deaf work, ask yourself, "What burden or vision has God given me to meet needs in my sphere of influence?" Assuming that our sphere of influence entails the deaf community, what kind of ministry would we begin today under God's guidance with reliance on his power?

The Burden and Vision to Minister

When we are determining our involvement with deaf work, whether within a church or out among individual members of the deaf community, our Christian motivation is usually linked to two important factors: *burden* and *need.* The nature of the *need* focuses our ministry. The *burden* is a growing conviction from God that he is calling *us* to respond in compassionate obedience to that need. In other words, to be burdened about some person or group of persons means we *make ourselves available before God to respond to that need.*

Often, as God prepares our hearts for ministry, he gives us a vision. He stimulates us by giving us a glimpse of what can be accomplished through and with him. When asked what she considered to be the greatest tragedy that could befall a person, Helen Keller responded, "To have sight but lack vision." We may have our minds full of facts and compiled statistics on deafness around the world, the types and causes of deafness, and language and cultural differences, but what God wants us to do is incorporate all these things into our "spiritual vision" and hold the torch of his Word high so others can catch sight of Jesus Christ. How is your spiritual vision?

WHERE DOES THE MINISTRY BEGIN?

Before beginning any type of Christian work among deaf people, establish a support group for prayer, accountability, and encouragement. Ministry is spiritual warfare. Front-line ministers need the prayer, support, encouragement, and discernment of like-minded people to have a meaningful impact. But beware the fiery darts of discouragement from the Author of Lies, the devil himself, who has no interest in new and exciting deaf ministries. Depend on that support group as the lifeline for your ministry.

Ultimately, ministry begins and ends with reliance on the Holy Spirit. No matter how proficient we may be in the language of signs or how well accepted we are in the deaf community, the Holy Spirit *must* open the door. Each of us, then, must be completely open to the Holy Spirit's direction. Only God's Spirit can equip us with the sensitivity, courage, wisdom, and unconditional love needed to respond to the needs of deaf people.

The question I see facing the church on the threshold of the twenty-first century is whether the church will become increasingly occupied with its own survival and security or will instead be unleashed in mission and ministry. Will the church open itself up to those who may pose a slight inconvenience? Will the church strive to serve those who have special needs such as transportation, additional ramps, revised curriculum, or the language of signs?

The problem is neither scarcity of God's resources nor lack of opportunity. The question is whether we will allow the Holy Spirit to concentrate our motivation, vision, and commitment to ministry within our spheres of influence. As Joni Eareckson Tada travels the world, she challenges the church with these words:

> Who will touch the lives of "deaf people" for Christ? We hope you and your church will. As your congregation becomes equipped and trained to reach out to anyone with any kind of disability, whether visible or invisible, they will discover the joy of caring.

I challenge you: Equip your hearts, your minds, and above all, your hands to go forth with the message of Jesus Christ. "I tell you, open your eyes and look at the fields! They are ripe for harvest" (John 4:35).

DISCERNING YOUR SPIRITUAL GIFTS

Teaching

Usually   Yes   No

———   ———   ———   1. Do you enjoy public speaking?
———   ———   ———   2. Do you like to discuss issues with others?
———   ———   ———   3. Do you organize your thoughts?
———   ———   ———   4. Do you enjoy the study of God's Word?
———   ———   ———   5. When problems arise, do you enjoy solving them?
———   ———   ———   6. Would you enjoy teaching?
———   ———   ———   7. Do you enjoy explaining things to people?
———   ———   ———   8. Do people seek your answers to questions or problems?
———   ———   ———   9. Have other people told you that you ought to teach?
———   ———   ———   10. Do you enjoy searching for answers to questions?

Serving

Usually   Yes   No

———   ———   ———   1. Do you find yourself sensitive to the needs of others?
———   ———   ———   2. When a job needs to be done, do you volunteer?
———   ———   ———   3. Do you enjoy finding jobs to do?
———   ———   ———   4. Do you seek praise when doing a job?
———   ———   ———   5. When asked to do a favor, do you mind doing it?
———   ———   ———   6. Do you enjoy doing tasks no one else will do?
———   ———   ———   7. Do you like to be asked to do a job?
———   ———   ———   8. Do you find satisfaction in doing things for others?
———   ———   ———   9. When a small task is not done, does this bother you?
———   ———   ———   10. Do you finish a task even though you may not be responsible for it?

Exhortation

Usually   Yes   No

———   ———   ———   1. Do you enjoy sharing someone else's personal problems?
———   ———   ———   2. Do you receive satisfaction when helping people with personal problems?
———   ———   ———   3. Does it bother you to deal with people who are depressed?
———   ———   ———   4. Do you enjoy encouraging people who are going through personal problems?
———   ———   ———   5. Are you a good listener?
———   ———   ———   6. Do people often express how much you have helped or encouraged them?
———   ———   ———   7. When a fellow believer has "sinned" or "fallen away," are you anxious to help him or her?

Showing Mercy

Usually	Yes	No

____ ____ ____ 1. Do you enjoy visiting the sick or disabled?

____ ____ ____ 2. Do you enjoy bringing encouragement and cheer to people in hospitals?

____ ____ ____ 3. Do you have a lot of compassion for people who are suffering?

____ ____ ____ 4. Would you like to have been a doctor or a nurse?

____ ____ ____ 5. Have you ever felt a special ministry toward the sick and suffering?

____ ____ ____ 6. Would you like a regular ministry to sick and shut-in people?

____ ____ ____ 7. When someone is suffering and shares it with you, do you seek to make them happy and cheerful?

____ ____ ____ 8. Would you enjoy spending time, money, and other resources to help people who are in physical need?

Ruling (Administration of people)

Usually	Yes	No

____ ____ ____ 1. Would you like to be the boss or president of your own company?

____ ____ ____ 2. Do you like making decisions?

____ ____ ____ 3. Do you prefer giving instructions to others?

____ ____ ____ 4. Is it easy for you to make decisions quickly?

____ ____ ____ 5. Do you handle problems with ease?

____ ____ ____ 6. Do you usually take the leadership in a group?

____ ____ ____ 7. Can you take pressure from others when they conflict with what you are planning or organizing?

____ ____ ____ 8. Do you have a discernment of people's needs, goals, and desires and could you devise the plans necessary to accomplish them?

____ ____ ____ 9. Do you enjoy motivating others?

____ ____ ____ 10. When asked to do a job, do you need specific directions before doing it?

Giving

Usually	Yes	No

____ ____ ____ 1. Do you find it easy to give your money or possessions to others without thought of what you will receive in return?

____ ____ ____ 2. When you give to people or projects, do you avoid publicity or letting anyone know you did it?

____ ____ ____ 3. Do you seek opportunities to give without being asked?

____ ____ ____ 4. Do you enjoy giving regardless of the response of those who receive?

_____ _____ _____ 5. When someone is in need, do you think of sending the person money?

_____ _____ _____ 6. Do you usually give without taking a lot of time for the decision?

_____ _____ _____ 7. When you give, are you unconcerned about whether you can afford it?

_____ _____ _____ 8. Are you really thrilled when someone asks you to help financially?

_____ _____ _____ 9. Are you offended by financial appeals, either public or private?

_____ _____ _____ 10. Are you careful about keeping records of what you have given?

Faith

Usually   Yes   No

_____ _____ _____ 1. Would you rather bring your needs to God in prayer than talking to others about them?

_____ _____ _____ 2. Do you find it easy to trust God for your physical needs?

_____ _____ _____ 3. Do you find it easy to ask God unconditionally for things?

_____ _____ _____ 4. Do you find satisfaction in seeing God answer prayer?

_____ _____ _____ 5. Do you enjoy receiving prayer requests?

_____ _____ _____ 6. Do you see difficulties as opportunities for God to display his glory?

_____ _____ _____ 7. When you have a vision to do certain things, do you follow through until they are accomplished?

Wisdom

Usually   Yes   No

_____ _____ _____ 1. Do you find it easy to reduce biblical truths to principles?

_____ _____ _____ 2. If there is a dispute among believers, do you find yourself clarifying the issues and helping to reconcile the two sides?

_____ _____ _____ 3. Is it easy for you to clarify people's problems for them and to offer solutions?

_____ _____ _____ 4. Do you get impatient with people who do not get the point quickly?

_____ _____ _____ 5. Is it easy to find illustrations for truths that you want to communicate?

_____ _____ _____ 6. Do people often come to you for solutions?

Knowledge

Usually   Yes   No

_____ _____ _____ 1. Do you enjoy attacking biblical problems and researching the issues?

——— ——— ——— 2. Do you get so involved in the mechanics of research that you forget about having to communicate it?

——— ——— ——— 3. Do you enjoy reading scholarly works and debates on biblical issues?

——— ——— ——— 4. Do you enjoy defending your position on a theological or scholarly issue?

——— ——— ——— 5. Is it difficult to communicate your excitement over some insight that you have discovered in the Word?

——— ——— ——— 6. Would you enjoy doing research rather than pastoral work?

Administration (of things)

Usually   Yes   No

——— ——— ——— 1. Do you like things organized?

——— ——— ——— 2. Do you like others organized?

——— ——— ——— 3. Are you a disciplined person?

——— ——— ——— 4. Do you enjoy seeing the successful operation of an activity?

——— ——— ——— 5. Do you want a room to be neat and things in their place?

——— ——— ——— 6. Do you like to help others organize themselves and their property?

——— ——— ——— 7. Do you see past the surface of an activity to the broader picture of details that make everything fit together?

——— ——— ——— 8. Can you see weaknesses in the organization of activities, ministries, and the like?

——— ——— ——— 9. Do you want time to be budgeted properly?

——— ——— ——— 10. Are you basically a structured person?

(A more complete questionnaire and a definition of results may be obtained by requesting the "Wagner Modified Houts Questionnaire" from the Charles E. Fuller Institute, P.O. Box 91990, Pasadena, CA 91109.)

THE PERFECTLY EQUIPPED INTERPRETER

*The following equipment is necessary for an interpreter to
do the best job:*

1. *EXTRA LARGE EAR . . . to hear the minister clearly.*
2. *TWO HEADS . . . one to listen to the minister and the
   other to formulate signs.*
3. *EXTRA LARGE HEAD . . . to contain large brain required
   to understand some ministers.*
4. *FIVE ARMS AND HANDS . . .*
   . . . two hands to interpret with
   . . . one hand to hold books, etc.
   *. . . two hands to chase "rabbits" which jump up in
   the middle of sermons.*
5. *EXTRA LONG LEGS . . . because tall people always sit
   in front and short people always sit in back.*
6. *BROAD SHOULDERS . . . to bear everyone's burdens.*
7. *THICK, HARD SKIN . . . because of "friends" who point
   out your faults . . . often.*
8. *PLENTY OF HAIR . . . so you can pull it out in
   frustration without ruining your appearance.*
9. *PERPETUAL SMILE . . . have this frozen on your face at
   the nearest freezer plant. You must not show
   disappointment, sadness, or when you are tired. If
   there is a blank look on your interpreter, it is because
   she has been interpreting for many years.*
10. *A TERRY CLOTH PAD ON THE SHOULDER . . . for
    people to cry on.**

*By Jerry Potter. Used by permission.

FOUR

The Church Interpreter: God's Messenger

*For we do not preach [interpret] ourselves, but
Jesus Christ as Lord, and ourselves as your servants
for Jesus' sake.*   **—2 CORINTHIANS 4:5**

T HE INTERPRETER is the major link between the deaf and hearing worlds. What a responsibility! Interpreters in the church must understand and accept that responsibility along with the mandate to share God's infinite love and life-changing message through their hands and conduct.

The interpreter's role is much like that of a pastor. He is "out in front" with many eyes on him. Flaws as well as strengths are sure to be seen inside and out. For those interested in beginning a deaf ministry, it is important to define the responsibilities that come with accepting the call to interpret. Many times a pastor will seize a layperson's offer to begin interpreting the worship services: "What a great idea! Sure! Can you start this Sunday?" But there are qualifications that must be met for meaningful interpretation to occur.

THE INTERPRETER'S MOTIVATION

Before we can share God's love, we must first possess it. I am a firm believer that only those who have accepted Christ Jesus as their personal Lord and Savior should be placed in the interpreter's seat during a worship service. While this qualification applies to almost every responsibility in the church setting, it is especially important that the interpretation of the gospel not be entrusted to the hands of a nonbeliever.

Once, while I was ministering in India with the Celebrant Singers and Orchestra, we were singing before a crowd of more than four thousand Hindus and needed the help of a Hindi translator. One was secured by our non-Christian sponsor. We proceeded to share the message, "Jesus is the way, the truth, and the life, and no one comes unto the Father except by him. He is the one and only Lord, and you must accept Him as your one and only Lord . . . No other gods before him. . . ."

We were thrilled to see hundreds respond to an invitation to ask Christ into their lives. There was only one problem. Those who responded to "the call" wanted to accept Jesus as *one of their gods,* not as *the* one and only God. Whether the interpreter changed the message intentionally or whether his interpreting skill was inadequate, the result was that the gospel had been distorted. It taught us an invaluable lesson: When choosing interpreters, make *certain* they are mature believers and are competent in the language interpreted.

This lesson holds true with sign language interpreters. We entrust the gospel to their hands. When I first began interpreting for my church, I often became lost during a sermon taken from the Old Testament. Having never studied it before, I would miss certain words and concepts, and this meant that deaf members missed the message! Finally I enrolled in an Old Testament Bible study, and what an improvement!

Consistent study of God's Word produces an interpreter knowledgeable in religious terms, names, doctrine, and Bible stories. This is vital to church interpreting. The best way to be prepared is to become involved in a Bible study and personally read and study the Scriptures daily.

I stress Bible knowledge, but it cannot supercede a genuine desire to share the love of Christ. Many times deaf people look to interpreters for living examples of God's love. Croft M. Pentz states in *Ministry to the Deaf:*

> Your life will be the greatest sermon or lesson you will teach.
> In other words, what you are is more important than what you
> do. The people will forget your words, but not how you live. A

happy, energetic, dedicated person will win many deaf people to Christ.[1]

How true! I encourage you to live holy lives that God's love can be seen in you.

THE INTERPRETER'S TEMPTATION

Church interpreters are the most visible members of a deaf ministry team. They are placed in the center physically every week. At first, even the hearing members of the congregation will focus on them, and there will be much praise and encouragement for their "ministry." This attention is short-lived, however. Soon the congregation grows accustomed to seeing the interpreter and then may take him or her for granted, just as they do the organist or even the pastor.

I have personally seen many interpreters quickly "burn out" because they started with the wrong motivation. It is tempting to desire the spotlight, to imagine yourself signing in front of the congregation. You may think, "What a great way to practice my signs!" But a church service is not the place to "train." When the interpreter's motives are impure, it is the deaf worshipers who suffer. When the interpreter's priorities are out of order and based on selfish motives, deaf people experience the following feelings:

- Confusion (from unskilled interpreting), which turns to frustration and finally deep disappointment
- Distrust of church groups in general (causing some people to try church only once)
- Apprehension or suspicion toward becoming further involved with the church's current or future ministries
- Lack of trust and commitment, with the thought, "This ministry will dissolve as rapidly as it appeared, just like so many before."

The result is reproach brought to the gospel and havoc in the church.

In her paper "The Expectations of an Interpreter," Meriam Johnson poses several questions:

Are you just as content sitting with the group as when interpreting? Are you in a church to work or to worship? You must accept the responsibility of interpreting exactly as you would any other position in a local church, as a service for the Lord that is neither more nor less important than the nursery worker or the Sunday School Superintendent. Each has a place to fill and interpreting happens to be yours. Given another set of circumstances or another church, you would serve in another capacity. This is essential to a truly humble spirit, and the only way to avoid personality conflicts and jealousies that have a tendency to develop among interpreters, perhaps because the interpreter is seen in a more conspicuous way, and is subjected to more public attention and praise than other teachers and officers.[2]

It is essential for interpreters to regard their attitude faithfully every time they are in the interpreting seat. When given praise, direct it to where it belongs—to the Lord. God desires to use humble interpreters who are willing to surrender all and offer their hands as a living sacrifice. The Lord uses such hands in mighty ways.

THE INTERPRETER'S RESPONSIBILITIES

A love for the Lord and a pure heart come first, but alone they are not enough to carry out the ministry of interpreting. The interpreter must be proficient in two languages: ASL and English. It is disastrous for the novice signer to put himself in an interpreting situation that is far beyond his skill level; the greatest harm will be done to the deaf people themselves. Let me give two examples.

The pastor of a particular church was challenging his congregation to "share" Jesus with other people. The interpreter proceeded to sign that the people needed to "cast out" Jesus to other people. The signs for *share* and *cast out* are very similar, but the messages they impart are very different.

In another circumstance, the pastor stated that the blood of Jesus is "precious"—an idea expressed by forming two *f*'s rolling up to meet as a circle. Instead of bringing the *f*'s together, the interpreter brought them up and then dropped them down, signing that the blood of Jesus was "worthless." A slight slip of the sign completely changed the pastor's message! This type of mistake spreads delusion among deaf people, not to mention heresy. As interpreters we *must* handle the Word of God accurately.

Memorizing signed vocabulary and signing it is not too difficult for most people. Even my daughter at age two had a signing vocabulary of 350 words. The ability to visualize and comprehend sign language with an occasional finger-spelled word at seventy miles per hour, however, is not easily gained. The best way to become fluent in sign language is to spend a great deal of time with deaf people in their own setting.

Interacting with the deaf community allows us to become familiar with new styles and techniques developing in American Sign Language. We will observe handshapes and sizes we have never seen before. The signs we practiced for hours in the classroom will come alive for us. Deaf people are the best teachers of their own language, so we should accept their suggestions and criticism. Maintain an open mind and avoid conveying a know-it-all attitude that is often labeled "the Beginning Sign Language Student Syndrome." The more we interact with deaf people, the more humility we will acquire, which is healthy for everyone. Keep in mind that our sign language skills are determined by the effort we put forth. How much effort are you putting forth at the present time?

An interpreter's involvement with the deaf community is essential for both ASL fluency and for an effective *ministry*. Once we begin to experience this culture, we begin to appreciate not only its language, but also its goals, environment, struggles, and commonalities. The majority of deaf people will welcome us with open arms and share their lives with us along with their language. Most are pleased to see their co-workers, neighbors, sales clerks, and newfound friends eager to learn sign language. Those who make the effort to walk through the "glass wall" that separates many deaf from their hearing peers are warmly welcomed.

It is important to approach the deaf community with love and respect, eager for what they have to offer us instead of our being concerned with what we can do for them. Do not approach the deaf community if you are drawn only by its novelty. Deaf people are very perceptive and will immediately detect the level of our sincerity.

As a representative of the church, we have an additional responsibility for acquainting ourselves with the deaf world. As interpreters we must express the needs of the deaf members of the church to its leaders. Frequently, those who are silent are overlooked. Encourage the pastors to remember to include deaf people in the worship services. They can testify, pray, read Scripture, preach, sign songs, usher— everything.

Now that we realize the responsibilities (and rewards) of interaction with the deaf community, where do we start? Get to know the leaders of the deaf community. Attend club meetings, bowling leagues, and holiday parties. Get involved with the local deaf advocacy organizations in the community. Participate in the National Association for the Deaf (NAD) or the Registry of Interpreters for the Deaf (RID), vocational rehabilitation programs, local deaf schools, and sign language programs at nearby colleges. All these provide an opportunity for us as the church representatives to establish trustworthiness in the eyes of the deaf community. Don't attend these functions to "preach at" the people, but use them to develop a rapport and, it is hoped, many meaningful friendships. This will not happen overnight. Relationships take lots of time to develop. By spending time with deaf people, we step into a rich and beautiful culture.

THE INTERPRETER'S ACTIVITIES

Many people assume that the interpreter just walks in, listens to the words spoken or sung, and then interprets. Nothing is further from the truth. A competent interpreter will spend a great deal of time translating music and sermons. The effectiveness of our part in the worship service depends on the amount of time we have to prepare, translate, and practice communicating the Scripture and songs.

The pastor or minister of music needs to plan ahead if he or she wants the deaf members to enjoy music in the worship service. We will need the hymns, special music, choruses, poems, choir anthems, and other materials several days prior to the worship service. Perhaps someone could even have all the lyrics typed, double-spaced, ready for us to translate. Keep all typed translations on file, ready to use again later.

Scripture passages, liturgies, and responsive readings should also be typed out ahead of time. The pastor must keep in mind the need to prepare the interpreter for very symbolic messages if he wants the deaf congregation to grasp his teaching.

Proper attire for the church event is important for an interpreter. Wear a solid color, with no distracting jewelry. If you really want to become an effective professional interpreter, adopt a conservative style of dress, upholding the dignity of the profession and not drawing undue attention to yourself. A pioneer in the field of interpreting has said, "You can always tell a professional interpreter by his or her wardrobe. The closet is lined with solid colors."

The interpreter arrives early enough before the service to set up the order of worship. Make sure you have a music stand on which to set your translations. Proper lighting must be arranged. The best lighting should be above the interpreter, not above the congregation, and most important, it should not be glaring into the people's eyes. Is the deaf section appropriate to the needs of the deaf people and reserved regularly? Can the deaf people see the interpreter and pastor simultaneously? Good preparation makes a good ministry.

Interpreters, however, must also be flexible. There will sometimes be a last-minute solo, a change of Scripture text, an unexpected speaker, or—worse yet—a film! Interpreters must accept the changes, remain calm, do the best they can—and pray! The Holy Spirit can do wonderful things through our hands. Trust God to work through you when a last-minute change occurs.

THE INTERPRETER'S CO-WORKERS

Many times interpreters develop a feeling that they are *indispensable.* When "the interpreter" is absent from church, where does that leave the deaf members of the congregation who have come eager to "hear" God's Word? It is important to establish at the beginning of a deaf ministry that even without *our* presence, the ministry of interpreting will take place. In her paper, "Ideas for a Total Ministry," Jan Kanda states:

> A good leader is one who, when absent, is not missed. A
> good leader is one who takes the painstaking time to train,
> teach and guide others to do the work. If, when that person
> moves or becomes ill for a length of time, the program
> screeches to a halt or falls apart, the world will then know
> that one person was busy with all the doing and no one
> profited on a long-term basis by his or her presence in that
> place of responsibility.[3]

It is often easier to do something yourself than to teach someone else to do it. But with planning and effort it is possible to have an ongoing training program for new interpreters and leaders.

The best (and most overlooked) method of recruiting people to train for interpreting is to pray for them to be "called." Be cautious when recruiting. Accept only those who come to you *eagerly.* Among those, look for the gift of interpreting. Many have the knowledge and skill of signing, but lack the ability to interpret. Discuss thoroughly with them their vision for the ministry and how it aligns with your own. Workers you can choose with confidence will learn faster and contribute more to the interpreting ministry.

Once you have selected co-workers, you must allow them, at your discretion, to interpret on various occasions. If possible, be present at such times to offer encouragement and meet them after the service to offer suggestions for improvement. This is one of the most effective ways to teach.

An ideal situation is to have at least two interpreters available during a Sunday morning worship service. One can interpret the announcements and music; the other, the sermon. The assignments can vary according to the structure of the service.

Eventually your church may have several interpreters available. One should be selected as team coordinator, whose major responsibility will be to arrange a monthly schedule that assigns each interpreter to specific events. The deaf members of the church should have the freedom to attend any church function with the security of knowing that an interpreter will be present. Coordinating each interpreter's schedule with the worship times, business meetings, special music presentations, and other events takes a great deal of organization and commitment. Yet, with interpreting needs met, the coordinator is able to participate in worship with the deaf and observe their responses. In this way the coordinator can detect unmet needs and evaluate the ministry. The ministry will be enhanced, and a rotation of available interpreters will decrease the burn-out rate.

THE INTERPRETER'S CHALLENGE

The interpreter faces the challenge to step back and allow the church to step forward. The interpreter's role has many facets. It involves study, prayer, time, and emotional commitment. It requires teamwork with the church staff, being sensitive to the deaf community's needs, deaf advocacy, and above all else, a servant's heart.

Begin now to think of yourself as not only an ambassador for Christ, but an envoy between cultures. There is no greater joy than when the middleman—the interpreter—is eliminated and real eye-to-eye communication takes place between deaf and hearing members of the church. When a hearing person taps you, the interpreter, on the shoulder and says, "Please tell the deaf person that . . . ," it is time for you to back away, allowing eye contact between the hearing and deaf persons themselves. Interpret when necessary, but allow rapport to develop between the hearing and deaf people. We as ministers are there to serve only as transmitters of information.

For example, in one church of which I was a member, the pastor's wife, Gloria, always sat in the deaf section directly behind a deaf person. Whenever the pastor said, "Please turn around and welcome someone this morning," Gloria was ready to greet the people in front of her. It always thrilled my heart to observe her signing, "Good morning! How are you?" in her own exuberant style. The love she showed to those deaf members was unforgettable.

Gloria took a risk by sitting in the deaf section of that church, but she communicated God's love with one simple phrase. She also reached out in other ways, such as inviting the entire group to her home for dinner. And who was the only hearing person invited to a deaf member's birthday party? You guessed it—good old Gloria!

Gloria was not an interpreter, nor did she desire to be. She was just willing to be sensitive, to communicate, and to serve in her silent way. As interpreters we must strive for excellent communication, and sometimes that means backing off and encouraging those with little or no sign language skills to communicate God's love with a smile or a handshake.

As Christians first and interpreters second, let us make God the focus of our lives. Let us reflect him through what we are and what we do. Interpret, yes, but at the same time realize that without God's empowerment, we are like a clanging gong or a crashing cymbal. The most we can be is faithful servants of God, eager to sign worthy of his calling. We want to hear those joyous words, "Well done, good and faithful servant." They may even be signed to us!

■ ■ ■

INTERPRETERS ARE HUMAN

Interpreters are human, believe it or not, much like the rest of us. They come in both sexes and in various sizes, but they are usually ladies, who are always most attractive.

Interpreters are found everywhere:
 in court—in the doctor's office
 in churches—in homes
 at weddings and at funerals.

They are usually around where there are deaf people, often relating all sides of a three-way conversation.

> *Interpreters must have*
> the wisdom of Solomon
> the disposition of a lamb
> the endurance of steel
> and the grace of a kitten.

They interpret for a deaf mother whose son is being questioned at Juvenile Hall or being honored at school. Too often they must interpret for a deaf child whose parents have made no effort to learn to communicate with him in sign language.

An interpreter who does well "has such beautiful motions." When he gets confused and flustered he "disrupts the whole meeting."

At church he interprets the invocation . . . the call to worship . . . the congregational songs . . . the announcements . . . that evening the pastor is away so the interpreter is faced with a substitute who st-st-stutters, has an *Irish* brogue, and didn't have time to prepare so he "J-u-s-t t-a-l-k-s."

> *Interpreters are asked* questions
> about their ability to read lips
> or "can you read Braille?"
> or why don't all deaf people use a hearing aid
> "like my uncle"?

And then, most people assume interpreters are making some kind of manual *short hand* or *semaphore* with their hands instead of using a distinct language with all the nuances and difficulties faced by the expert translators at the United Nations building.

> *Interpreters are at work*
> in any kind of weather—any time of day
> any season of the year

hearing excuses why others couldn't come: "it rained," "the meeting was too late at night," and "it's Christmas time."

An interpreter who stands up in the front of the audience seeks attention. If he sits to interpret he doesn't put himself into his work.

If he speaks out during the meeting he is out of his professional role. If he keeps silent he is not supportive.

If he has been interpreting for only a few years he lacks experience. If he has been interpreting for many years he is in a rut and old fashioned.

If he uses a lot of facial expression he distracts from the speaker. If he doesn't he is a dead-panned puppet.

If he doesn't train others to help him he thinks no one is as good as he is. If he does train others he is trying to pass himself off as an expert.

Interpreters like:
    cooperation—appreciation
    and seeing deaf people become self-sufficient.

They dislike: to be conspicuous, to be imposed upon, and to face the ignorance of those who know nothing about deafness or see the interpreter as just a "machine."

Interpreters are human—
    usually very busy humans
    occasionally very tired humans
    seldom very unhappy humans.*

---

*By George B. Joslin, in the newsletter of the Communication Service for the Deaf (Larry Puthoff, editor), vol. 2, no. 3 (15 November 1987). Used by permission.

LET YOUR SPIRIT SHOUT

■ ■ ■

Together we watch the trees sway in the wind
    You tell me it sighs in the branches
We watch the breakers roll up to the shore
    You tell me they thunder on the sand
We see a meadowlark lift its head to sing
    You tell me its cries are like distant chimes
My friends smile as they talk to me
    You tell me they speak in tones of love.

    I cannot hear the sighing of the wind
        I do not hear the pounding of the surf
        I cannot hear the singing of the birds
        I will never hear the tones of love.

Yours is a world of music, mine of silence.
Though ears are closed and cannot hear
A shout from within will reach His throne.

Come rejoice with me, for Christ is here
To warm your heart and guide you through eternity
So, come now, sign a song of joy with me
Lift up your hands, cry out to Him.

                    *Let Your Spirit Dance.**

*By Mark Maupin. Copyright © 1989. Used by permission.

FIVE

Sign to the Lord
a New Song

*Sing [sign] to the LORD a new song,
for he has done marvelous things.*

—PSALM 98:1

D O DEAF PEOPLE enjoy music? As hearing people, we are drawn
into worship by a choir or a solo or congregational singing.
Sometimes we are brought to conviction and deeper commitment to
the Lord through music. But are deaf people able to be just as inspired
through music?

Vesta Bice, director of Deaf Opportunity Outreach (D.O.O.R.),
writes,

> Even though many deaf people have partial hearing and have
> experienced music to a degree, still they are more blessed
> and inspired when they can *see* the music and partially hear
> it. It makes what they can hear so much more vivid. For the
> profoundly deaf person with little or no residual hearing, try to
> create the same effect with the proper choice and use of
> signs. It is fantastic when the music becomes totally visual,
> and the deaf individual can *see* the message and feel the
> music from within. So let them *hear* the song, *understand*
> the song, and *feel* the song![1]

71

The signing of hymns, choruses, and solos is an important part of worship for deaf people. It must therefore be done with as much beauty and meaning as possible. Music sets the mood, influences our responses, moves our emotions, and prepares the heart and mind for worship. The mood that is set depends greatly on the interpreter.

THE INTERPRETER: A STUDENT OF MANY LANGUAGES

The interpreter of church music must study the English language, American Sign Language, and the Bible. It even helps to know a little Greek! Why? Because it is impossible to translate something into another language until we understand it in its original language. Before you even begin to translate music, be sure to have by your side a good dictionary and a thesaurus. You should take the following steps before beginning to translate:

- Read the entire song; *never* translate sentence by sentence or word for word.
- Ask yourself, what is the author saying? Is he expressing love, joy, sorrow, hate, or some other feeling?
- Determine who or what the author is talking about.

Just as English words must be understood before they can be signed, so too must religious terminology. Old English hymns must be studied and understood before they can be interpreted. William E. Davis gives an example using the hymn "Come Thou Fount":

In the line which reads,

"Here I raise mine Ebenezer,
hither by thy help I've come,"

neither raise nor Ebenezer can be signed with meaning unless
the interpreter knows that Ebenezer means "stone of help"
and was erected between Mizpah and Shen by Samuel with
the statement, "Hitherto has the Lord helped us," commemo-
rating Israel's defeat of the Philistines. So "raise" literally
means to establish or to build and "Ebenezer" means something like a monument or altar which symbolizes God's leadership and help up to that point.[2]

You may be thinking, "I just want to sign in front of the church, I don't want to study theology." Often God's message is found in hymns and anthems that contain direct quotations from the Scriptures. We as interpreters *must* be prepared regardless of the setting, whether educational, medical, or religious. The only way to have an accurate translation of the material presented is to have an accurate understanding of it. Remember 2 Timothy 2:15: "Do your best to present yourself to God as one approved, a workman who does not need to be ashamed and who correctly handles the word of truth."

As an interpreter of Christian music, I have always felt a double blessing when signing songs conceptually. After studying the true meaning of the songs and choosing accurate concepts, I experience a greater understanding. What a blessing to paint a picture in the air with my hands! The song becomes a true inner expression of praise to God powerfully manifested through the graphic means of sign language.

How do we learn to translate music conceptually? Skill comes only with a great deal of training and practice. It is essential to have instruction in American Sign Language and to understand its structure. We must be trained to think visually. For some, this foundation comes easily; for others the task may be more difficult. I see no need, however, to have a strong musical background in order to translate music. It is far more important to feel the music, know the language, know the people, and sign accordingly.

THE ART OF MAKING MUSIC VISUAL

For the purpose of this section, I will be focusing on the interpreter's role as a *sign-song leader.* Our first priority as "song leaders" is to give the deaf audience the pleasure and inspiration of "seeing music."

- Once you are ready to translate, read the song imaginatively, trying to build a mental image, recreating the song or story in your mind. I have heard of interpreters sketching a portrait of the song's meaning in order to group visual concepts together.
- Next, translate the song into visual signs. Paint a picture with your hands. A whole sentence may require only one sign. For example, "Jesus is all the world to me" can be translated *Jesus important.*

While it is not necessary to sing along, it is important to convey the *meaning* and the *message* of songs by using every available communication tool, not just signs. Moreover, we should only mouth words if the signed word is simultaneous with the spoken word, because it can be confusing when our hands say one thing and our mouths another.

For music, the movement of signs is much larger and becomes more rhythmic. The movements should flow with the music. Finger-spelling is reduced to the bare minimum. Signing songs requires much facial expression and body language. The difficulty lies in maintaining a balance between enough expression and too much. William Davis explains,

> The signing of church music must always be done in good taste. While many interpreters do a very good job in the area of music, there are, however, others who fall into one of two extremes. First, there is the interpreter who signs music in such a still and rigid manner that no one would ever suspect that there is an element of praise or warmth of devotion in the music. There is not much warmth and inspiration to be received from an icicle. Then, there is the interpreter at the other extreme. The interpreter always over-interprets and over-acts the music until you feel you are surely watching an old silent movie. The police have just taken the drunken father away to jail and the cruel landlord has evicted the helpless mother and twelve hungry children on a cold winter night. Now this is an exaggeration, to be sure, but it makes a point. The church is not a theater. There have been situations where deaf people surely have left the worship service sick to their stomachs instead of inspired and uplifted.[3]

As interpreters we must avoid the two extremes. The best way to do this is to practice signing before a mirror. Concentrate on worshiping the Lord instead of looking "worshipful." God is our only true audience, and his interest lies in humble hands and hearts. I write this out of concern for the novice signer who enjoys receiving pats and praise from the hearing congregation. I was once there. There are always some in the hearing congregation who, enthralled and curious, flock forward to say how much you have blessed them (a possibility) and what a superbly flawless job you did interpreting the message (an impossibility). Before lapping up the praise, consider that the person giving the compliment has no sign language background; the compliments don't carry much weight. I have learned to think of these compliments as little flowers politely received. When I have gathered a bouquet, I hand them over to the Lord. I know how hard it can be to do this, but keep things in a *humble* perspective. The only audiences that count are the Lord and the deaf people he has called you to serve. Sign worthy of his praise!

THE PROCESS BEGINS

The interpreter who leads the deaf congregation in "singing" with her hands must do as much preparation as the minister of music or choir director who leads the hearing congregation in worship. Let's examine the preparation process for translating the music for a hypothetical church service. The hymns and worship choruses have been selected, and the text of special music has been turned in. The secretary has typed the music (double-spaced), so it can be in your hands by Friday morning. One of the pieces is a solo, "Lamb of God," written and composed by Twila Paris; a sign language translation is available on videotape from Deaf Missions.

In preparing the other music, you read through a song several times. If possible, you listen to the song on cassette tape, visualizing in your mind the true meaning. Next, you must begin choosing accurate concepts and interpreting the song's meaning into appropriate signs. After that you must fit the signed concepts to the music. When in doubt about translating an abstract concept, don't hesitate to ask your pastor, music minister, fellow interpreters, or sign language instructor. Two minds are better than one.

There are different kinds of songs and music, and they arouse different moods. When a song is soft and graceful, such as "Lamb of God," all the signs should be done softly and gracefully. If the song is bouncy, quick, and energetic, such as "This Is the Day," then the signs should show that mood. Try to create the same effect with your choice of signs. Again, give facial expressions appropriate to the mood of the song. Don't overdo it, but don't put your deaf congregation to sleep, either.

Keep these questions in mind when you are considering a song for translation:

- Does the song have few abstract concepts?
- Does the song have a smooth, graceful, definite beat?
- Does the song repeat verses? (Deaf people tend to enjoy short songs with repeated phrases that lend themselves to movement, such as "Love Lifted [Inspired] Me." Repetition also helps to clarify the meaning. Praise Songs recordings and tapes offered by Maranatha! Music are a good source of this kind of music.)
- Is the song's meaning easily made visual?
- Does the song have potential for choreography, dramatization, and visual aids (possibly during the interlude)?

- Does the song have a message or story (such as the Crucifixion) that the deaf member can easily relate to?
- Most important, does the song inspire and bless *me* when I sign it? (As a song-sign director, how can I inspire others if the song has not first touched me?)

THE OPPORTUNITY TO BE FLEXIBLE

There will be times when the pastor gives you a Scripture reading at the last minute or a hymn is changed or the soloist forgets to give you the words. Few churches are aware of the preparations an interpreter needs to make before a church service. You the interpreter must make those needs known and probably more than once. Remember, you may be pioneering a new ministry. You are not only the *interpreter,* but also the *educator* of the pastoral staff and laypeople of your church.

So flexibility is an asset to an interpeter. You find yourself without a hymn text or the words to a solo, and you're beginning to worry. This is your opportunity, first, to *pray* and trust God, and then to keep calm and under control.

When you are signing a song with little or no preparation, you will have a tendency to sign less conceptually and follow the English word order. Perhaps you are very proficient at listening to an English phrase, mentally translating the abstract thought into a beautiful concept, and flashing it out on your hands in less than two seconds. But this skill level is rare. If we don't have it, we mustn't fret. We have to sign the song to the best of our ability. Afterward, request that the words be typed so that you can translate it properly and add it to your binder of translated songs. The next time the song is used, you will be prepared and confident.

SAMPLE TRANSLATIONS

It is important to keep in mind the language level of the deaf group we are interpreting for. So we begin by assessing the audience. Which of the following do they prefer?

- ASL translation (more conceptual)
- Signed Exact English translation (exact words and order)
- Pidgin English translation (combination of the above)

We must know our audience, then proceed to meet their needs in making God's message via music more worshipful and pleasurable. We should use our own judgment in determining whether it is best to sign the abstraction exactly as it appears in the language, modify it slightly, or sign the literal meaning instead of the abstraction. Let me reinforce that statement with some examples.

> I once was lost but now am found,
> was blind but now I see.
> —From "Amazing Grace"
> John Newton

If signed literally, this verse could cause some confusion, because I do not intend it to mean that I am physically blind or physically lost. Terms such as *lost, found, blind,* and *see* are abstract in that they have figurative meanings. There are several ways to conceptualize this phrase and clarify its true meaning. We could translate the phrase as follows:

English	Translation
I once was	PAST, ME
lost	SINNER
but now	BUT NOW
am found	SAVED
was	[not applicable]
blind	ME CONFUSE
but now	NOW
I see	UNDERSTAND [positive head shake]

The final sign translation is PAST, ME SINNER, BUT NOW SAVED, ME CONFUSE, NOW UNDERSTAND. This is a very basic translation. The translation may vary according to our skill level. There are other concepts and signs that could be used without changing the writer's intent. So be creative, think how *you* can best convey the song and message to the deaf congregation so that they can visually receive the song's meaning.

Let's practice more translating. Remember that the translations presented here are suggestions, not fixed forms. In my classes, students type the writer's lyrics double- or triple-spaced and in the spaces between lines write the translation in another color of ink. As you study these translations, remember—think pictures.

O God, Our Help in Ages Past

O God, our help in ages past,
Our hope for years to come,
Our shelter from the stormy blast,
And our eternal home.

—Isaac Watts

English	Translation
O God, our help	O GOD, OUR HELP
in ages past	UP TILL NOW
our hope	OUR HOPE
for years to come	FOR FUTURE
our shelter	OUR PROTECT [agent ending]
from the stormy blast	DURING TROUBLE
and our eternal home	GIVE [agent ending] HEAVEN

This method of translating songs may be new to you. That's why I use the expression "the opportunity to be flexible." If you feel this method of translating songs can benefit and enhance the deaf congregation's worship and their comprehension of church music, some more examples may prove helpful:

Holy, Holy, Holy

Holy, holy, holy, Lord God Almighty!
Early in the morning our song shall rise to Thee;
Holy, holy, holy! merciful and mighty!
God in three persons, blessed Trinity!
—Reginald Heber

English	Translation
Holy, holy, holy	HOLY, HOLY, HOLY
Lord God Almighty	LORD GOD STRONG
early in the morning	SUN RISE
our song shall rise to Thee	PRAISE YOU, WILL
Holy, holy, holy	HOLY, HOLY, HOLY,
merciful and mighty	MERCY AND STRONG
God in three persons	FATHER, JESUS, HOLY SPIRIT
blessed Trinity	BLESSED TRINITY

Deuteronomy 6:17

Ye shall diligently keep the commandments of the LORD your God, and his testimonies, and his statutes, which he hath commanded thee (KJV).

English	Translation
Ye shall	YOU [point forward]
diligently keep	EAGER OBEY
the commandments of the LORD	COMMANDMENTS FROM LORD
your God	GOD
and his testimonies	AND HIS [flat hand up] TEACH
and his statutes	AND HIS [flat hand up] LAW
which he hath	HE [point up] FINISH
commanded thee	COMMANDED YOU

O How He Loves You and Me!

Jesus to Calvary did go,
His love for mankind to show;
What He did there brought hope from despair;
O how He loves you,
O how He loves me,
O how He loves you and me!

—Kurt Kaiser*

English	Translation
Jesus to Calvary did go	JESUS CROSS—CRUCIFY
His love to mankind to show	HIS LOVE FOR PEOPLE (GIVE—OUT)
What He did there	CRUCIFY
brought hope from despair	CAUSE SORROW, BECOME HOPE
Oh, how He loves you	TRUE HE LOVES YOU
Oh, how He loves me	TRUE HE LOVES ME [honorific]
Oh, how He loves you and me	MUCH HE LOVES YOU AND ME

*Words and music by Kurt Kaiser. Copyright © 1975 by Word Music, Inc., Waco, Texas. Used by permission.

All the Way My Savior Leads Me

All the way my Savior leads me—
O the fullness of His love!
Perfect rest to me is promised
In my Father's house above.
When my spirit, clothed immortal,
Wings its flight to realms of day,
This my song through endless ages:
Jesus led me all the way;
This my song through endless ages:
Jesus led me all the way.

—Fanny J. Crosby

English	Translation
All the way	UP TILL NOW
my Savior leads me	SAVIOR LEADS ME
O the fullness of His love!	WONDERFUL HIS LOVE
Perfect rest	PEACE [for me]
to me is promised	HE [point up] PROMISED
in my Father's house above	FUTURE HEAVEN
When my spirit, clothed immortal	HAPPEN DIE BUT
wings its flight	GO–TO
to realms of day	HEAVEN WILL
This my song	MY SONG
through endless ages	FOREVER
Jesus led me	JESUS LED ME
all the way	CONTINUE
This my song	MY SONG
through endless ages	FOREVER
Jesus led me	JESUS LED ME
all the way	CONTINUE

Don't be disappointed if you feel totally confused at this point. Take heart. You may simply lack the vocabulary of signs necessary to comprehend these translations. I suggest you seek assistance from a respected, experienced Christian interpreter. Take a class in the translating of songs into sign language. These classes are often titled something like "Sign and Song."

For more experienced interpreters, or those who love a challenge, I include the translation of "Lamb of God" by Twila Paris (pages 82–83). I have chosen this song as my example because it lends itself to meaningful interpretation and involves the tips I mentioned earlier.

Remember that there are several ways to translate a song. This is my own translation; others might well improve on it. My goal is to underscore the importance of *conceptual accuracy* when translating from one language to another, especially in music. Our objective as interpreters is to convey as clearly and accurately as possible the gospel message so that the deaf congregation can not only grow spiritually, but also experience worship to its fullest.

A WORD OF ENCOURAGEMENT

A remarkable tribute to the power of interpreting the music of the church comes from Jerome Schein:

> That sign has a spiritual aspect should not surprise anyone, especially if one considers its use by silent religious orders and by priests in the education of deaf children. What must be seen to be fully appreciated, however, is its singular appropriateness for religious worship. The depth of expression that can be achieved by signing defies accurate description. The Academy Award won by Jane Wyman in 1948 for her portrayal of a deaf girl in *Johnny Belinda* undoubtedly owed much to her beautiful (and accurate) rendering of the Lord's Prayer in Ameslan [ASL].
>
> It is perhaps in the church service that the beauty of sign becomes most evident. Some churches have sign choirs. Watching the robed members sign in unison can be an awe-inspiring experience.[4]

Our interpreting a hymn in church on a typical Sunday morning may not achieve that height of grandeur, but the inherent beauty of communicating the gospel through sign language persists. Always recognize that interpreting skill is useless unless it is surrendered to

Lamb of God

Your only Son, no sin to hide,
But you have sent him from your side,
To walk upon this guilty sod
And to be called the Lamb of God.

Your gift of love they crucified.
They laughed and scorned him as he died.
The humble king they named a fraud
And sacrificed the Lamb of God.

CHORUS: O Lamb of God, sweet Lamb of God,
I love the holy Lamb of God.
O wash me in his precious blood,
My Jesus Christ, the Lamb of God.

I was so lost, I should have died,
But you have brought me to your side,
To be led by your staff and rod
And to be called a lamb of God.

O Lamb of God, sweet Lamb of God,
I love the holy Lamb of God.
O wash me in his precious blood,
'Til I am just a lamb of God.
O wash me in his precious blood,
My Jesus Christ, the Lamb of God.*

*Words and music by Twila Paris. Copyright © 1985 by Straight Way Music. (Used by permission of Gaither Copyright managment. (A video of a song translation is available from Deaf Missions, Council Bluffs, Iowa.)

WILLING   GIVE
GOD Your only Son, no sin to hide,
FOR SIN PEOPLE   JESUS   SELF   NO SIN
But you have sent him from your side,
(INDEX)   AMONG SIN PEOPLE
To walk upon this guilty sod
FORGIVE THEIR   SIN
And to be called the Lamb of God.

JESUS GOD'S GIFT   BUT
Your gift of love they crucified.
PEOPLE (PUT ON CROSS) CRUCIFY   MOCK
They laughed and scorned him as he died.
(FLAT HAND) (HUMBLE)   IGNORE   (LEFT HAND)
The humble king they named a fraud
REJECTED   (FLAT HANDS HONORIFIC)
And sacrificed the (Lamb of God.)

JESUS   GOD'S   GIFT
CHORUS: O Lamb of God, sweet Lamb of God,
JESUS
I love the holy Lamb of God.
MY   SIN   BLOOD   FORGIVE
O wash me in his precious blood,
GOD'S   GIFT
My Jesus Christ, the Lamb of God.

SELF SIN   (SEPARATE) ETERNAL
I was so lost, I should have died,
JESUS   FORGIVE   RE-UNITE
But you have brought me to your side,
HELP (FROM GOD)   INSPIRE (HERE-ON-OUT)
To be led by your staff and rod
BECOME   SUBMIT / SURRENDER
And to be called a lamb of God.

JESUS   GOD'S   GIFT
O Lamb of God, sweet Lamb of God,
JESUS
I love the holy (Lamb of God.)
MY   SIN   BLOOD   FORGIVE
O wash me in his precious blood,
HAPPEN CHANGE   ME
'Til I am just a lamb of God.
MY   SIN   BLOOD   FORGIVE
O wash me in his precious blood,
GOD'S   GIFT
My Jesus Christ, the Lamb of God.

God. There are many talented people who can sing and sign expertly, but because their hearts are not right, their message falls by the wayside.

Be an example to your deaf congregation by surrendering your hands, talents, and abilities to the Lord. Success comes from the Father; you and the deaf members of the church are all instruments of God. Pray diligently for every church service, for the testimony of the deaf members, and for guidance by the Spirit. Every opportunity for the interpreter is an opportunity to serve God. Approach each opportunity seriously and prayerfully, whether you are signing for two people or two hundred. Through the interpreter's actions and example, the deaf people can come to understand the high calling of being a Christian and find their *own* ways to serve the Lord.

> *But we have this treasure in jars of clay [Jesus in us] to show that this all-surpassing power is from God and not from us.* —2 CORINTHIANS 4:7

III

COMMUNICATING WITH DEAF PEOPLE

■ ■ ■

SILENCE AND SOUND

■ ■ ■

I have a friend,
I love so dear.
I'd love to tell her,
But she can't hear.

This friend of mine,
She is so sweet,
With a loving heart,
But she can't speak.

Her world of silence,
My world of sound—
There's a wall between
That must come down.

She is so patient,
So good, and kind,
While she helps me
Learn how to sign.

No more silence,
No more sound,
No more walls
*Where love abounds.**

*By Phyllis Rutherford McKinney. Copyright © 1987 by *Home Life Magazine* (October 1987).

SIX

Faith Comes
by Seeing ...

A RE YOU READY? Let's get down to the basics of American Sign Language, otherwise known as ASL. Lou Fant, who is known as "Mr. Sign Language," describes ASL in *The American Sign Language Phrase Book:*

> First of all, ASL is not to be confused with other sign systems. These systems put the English language into a manual-visual form; thus, they are called systems of Manually Coded English (MCE). ASL is *not* a way of coding English, but rather a language in and of itself. It differs from English in many respects, such as it has its own syntax, sentence construction, grammar, and word order.[1]

GOD'S WORD MADE VISUAL

Most languages are based on sound, and that's where ASL is unique. It is a language based on *sight.* ASL is a visual-spatial language. In learning this very expressive language, you must concentrate not only on basic hand movements, but also facial expressions, head movements, body movements, and the space around you, the signer.

The average deaf adult reads English on a fourth-grade level, but has a twelfth-grade comprehension level in his native language, ASL. Speech and the printed page are the methods most often used to convey the message of Jesus Christ, but this presents a problem for the prelingual deaf person who is totally dependent on sight and the language of signs for spiritual education and growth. Meeting the needs of deaf people entails more than a once-a-month potluck. It requires making God's message of love and salvation come alive visually. Make your signs as vivid as a picture, easy to grasp with the eyes, and graphic enough to give a clear impression.

There is this caution, however, that American Sign Language is not universal. Each country, as well as each culture within a country, has its own sign language and a set of signs that stem from indigenous customs and rituals.

A vivid example comes from Calcutta, India. There the sign for "girl" is simply touching the index finger slightly above the right nostril, symbolizing the nose ring often worn by Indian women. The sign for "boy" is the twisting of the mustache. These signs are appropriate for the Indian culture, but are very different from American signs. Nevertheless, the sign for "Jesus" (making symbolic nail holes in each palm with the middle finger of each hand) seems to be universal. And why not? He died for "everyone."

The following pages display basic religious ASL phrases. The purpose of these sentences is to enable us to reach out to deaf people who may have been overlooked and to communicate with them.

The "Additional Vocabulary" section contains numerous signs for you to learn and develop into your own ASL phrases. Remember, however, that signs do vary considerably around the country, so be sure to inquire into the religious signs commonly used in your locality.

What's the next step? Go ... use your sign language. As Ted Engstrom profoundly states in his book, *The Pursuit of Excellence:*

> A life of excellence takes work, perseverance, and discipline; but it's worth every ounce of sweat and determination. If you choose to let your talents slide, be ready to accept the harsh verdict of that ancient law: What you refuse to use, you will surely lose.[2]

Learning the basic conversational phrases in this book will open many doors to share God's love in ways you never thought possible. Yet this is only the beginning. Let's break down the communication barrier and sign, SIGN, SIGN![3]

Let's Communicate

YOU?   SIGN

DO YOU SIGN?

HELLO   HOW   YOU?   FINE

HELLO, HOW ARE YOU? ... FINE!

NAME   WHAT [SHRUG]

WHAT'S YOUR NAME?

HAPPY   MEET

I'M HAPPY TO MEET YOU.

GOOD   MORNING   WELCOME   CHURCH

GOOD MORNING! WELCOME TO CHURCH!

SURPRISE   SEE (YOU)   AGAIN

I'M SURPRISED TO SEE YOU AGAIN!

PLEASE   SIT [SEAT]   HERE

PLEASE HAVE A SEAT RIGHT HERE.

CHURCH   FINISH   YOU AND I   MEET

LET'S GET TOGETHER WHEN CHURCH IS OVER.

CHRIST AGENT YOU

ARE YOU A CHRISTIAN?

BAPTIZE FINISH YOU

HAVE YOU BEEN BAPTIZED?

CHURCH JOIN WHICH

WHAT CHURCH DO YOU BELONG TO?

EVERY SUNDAY	CHURCH	GO TO	ME

I ATTEND CHURCH EVERY SUNDAY.

DEAF	SUNDAY SCHOOL	START	NOW

DEAF SUNDAY SCHOOL IS STARTING IMMEDIATELY.

WANT?   JOIN   JESUS

BOOK   STUDY

WOULD YOU LIKE TO JOIN A BIBLE STUDY?

DEAF MUSIC GROUP (CHOIR)

WANT PARTICIPATE

WOULD YOU LIKE TO JOIN THE DEAF CHOIR?

PREACH (SERMON) ME INTERPRET WILL

I WILL INTERPRET THE SERMON.

JESUS   BOOK

FOR   DEAF   HAVE

DO YOU HAVE THE DEAF VERSION OF THE BIBLE?

WORSHIP   GOD   IMPORTANT   TRUE

IT IS VERY IMPORTANT TO WORSHIP GOD.

DEAF

PREACH
(PREACHER)

DEAF

MISSION
(MISSIONARY)

TRUE

NEED

**THERE IS A GENUINE NEED FOR DEAF MISSIONARIES
AND DEAF PASTORS.**

OUR   GOAL   ESTABLISH

DEAF   CHURCH

OUR GOAL IS TO ESTABLISH A DEAF CHURCH.

SEE YOU   NEXT   SUNDAY   TAKE CARE

I'LL SEE YOU NEXT SUNDAY! TAKE CARE OF YOURSELF.

ADDITIONAL VOCABULARY

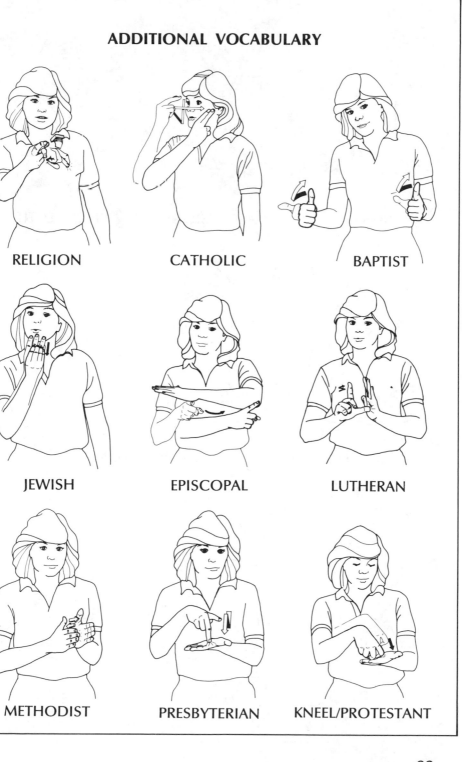

RELIGION

CATHOLIC

BAPTIST

JEWISH

EPISCOPAL

LUTHERAN

METHODIST

PRESBYTERIAN

KNEEL/PROTESTANT

BLESS   ASCENSION   RESURRECTION

(a) HELL   (b) HELL

FAITH   THINE   PITY/MERCY

GRAVE   AMEN   PRAY

ANGEL

HEAVEN

MINISTRY

CHAPTER

VERSE

CELEBRATE   SON   PROPHECY

VISION/DREAM   ETERNAL

CRUCIFY   SAVE/SALVATION

THOU

PRIEST
[One or two hands]

SATAN/EVIL

GLORY

PRAISE

TITHE

TEMPLE

VIRGIN

ATHEIST

CROSS   SOUL   COMMANDMENT

SIN   FUNERAL   FORGIVE

LIFE/LIVE   LORD   TRINITY

THE MANUAL ALPHABET

F-I-N-G-E-R–S-P-E-L-L-I-N-G can totally frustrate a novice signer. You may at first see this phenomenon fleeting through the air at an incomprehensibly fast rate of speed. Let me assure you, finger-spelling is easier to do than to read. Developing finger-spelling, or the manual alphabet, is necessary to communicate with deaf people. It is often used with proper names and when there is no sign for a particular idea.

To master the art of finger-spelling, we must form good habits from the start. How do you begin? First, take a deep breath, shake your hand out, and *relax your fingers.* Try stretching and bending your fingers so they will fall easily into the proper hand shapes. Are your knuckles white? You may still be a little tense.

Next, *relax your arms and shoulders.* Rid yourself of all tension; it can be an obstacle to forming clear letters. Let your arms hang down with the elbows at your side and the hands slightly in front of your body. Don't let the elbows start to move away from your side or rise upward. Picture your hands and upper chest within an imaginary "window." Strive to keep your hands comfortably within that window.

Rhythm is a very important quality to develop in finger-spelling. You may be thinking, "That's just great! I can't even keep the cadence of my own heartbeat, much less keep a rhythm with my fingers!" When a finger-spelled word is done with a repetitious motion and in a regular and harmonious pattern, it is considered *rhythmical spelling.* This does not mean that you bounce your hand; rather, hold it steadily in one place, stay within that imaginary window, and "let your fingers do the talking."

Remember, a slow rhythmic pattern is more desirable than a fast erratic one. Speed is not the goal. The key to *effective* communication is a paced, clear, smooth style of finger-spelling. One aid for developing a rhythmic style of finger-spelling is to practice with a metronome.

For good communication, mouth the words (not letters) that you finger-spell. As you finger-spell a word, say the entire word. For example, in spelling D-E-A-F, do not say the letters, but pronounce "deaf." Deaf people are taught to lipread words, not letters. When we both finger-spell and pronounce the word, the actions complement each other and convey a clear and accurate message. This takes practice and timing, but you can develop the skill if you practice finger-spelling and pronouncing words simultaneously from the beginning.

What about finger-spelling long words? You will inevitably encounter some. With these, think *syllables.* Pronounce the word syllable by

THE MANUAL ALPHABET

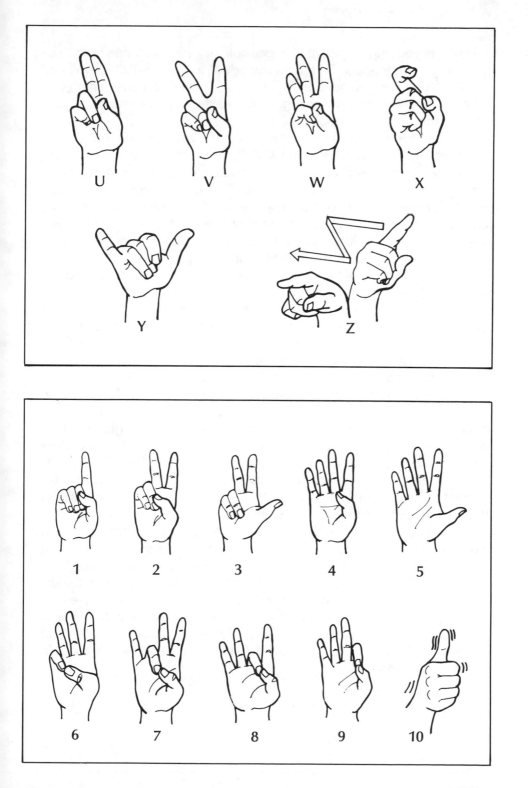

syllable as you finger-spell it. For example, for the word *endeavor,* say "en" as you finger-spell E-N, then say "dev" as you spell D-E-A-V, and finish with 'or" as you spell O-R. There is no need to pause after each syllable; keep the rhythm flowing. Double letters can be moved slightly to the side.

Begin learning the first three letters of the manual alphabet, A-B-C. Then immediately begin spelling C-A-B, pronouncing the word "cab" (aloud or silently). Add the letter "D," then spell D-A-D, saying "dad." With the next letter, "E," you can spell B-E-D while mouthing "bed." You might want to try finger-spelling the words from a simple, repetitive children's book. Then continue practicing your finger-spelling as you read the newspaper, listen to the radio, or watch television. Spell street signs or billboards, and work at breaking longer words into syllables. Practice regularly. Consistent practice is essential to developing good finger-spelling.

I repeat, finger-spelling is much easier than reading for deaf people. We must train our eyes to receive those fleeting letters and become less dependent on our ears. Reading and comprehending sign language require turning off the ears and turning on the eyes.

I watched an interesting example of this as I was finger-spelling the word *elephant* to my seven-year-old daughter. She immediately began to sound out the syllables "ell-e-fant." This came naturally to her, because that is the exact method by which she is being taught to read at school. She was looking for "*el*" on my hands, the same way she sounds out "*el*" on a page. Reading finger-spelling phonetically develops effective comprehension, and from the start you should strive to read syllables more than letters. Attempt to grasp parts of words with the aim of putting together a whole word.

Find someone to learn and practice finger-spelling with you. You might think of practicing before a mirror, but since you already know what you're going to finger-spell, your eyes are not getting the disciplined training needed to read both sign language and finger-spelling extemporaneously. So it is better to get a partner (preferably deaf), "turn off" your voice, and "turn on" the wavelengths between your eyes and your brain. Then practice, practice, practice. See and comprehend those beautiful L-E-T-T-E-R-S—or better yet, "words" in the manual alphabet.

HELP ME
MAKE A CHANGE

■ ■ ■

Dear Lord,
You know I'm not perfect
   and never will be.
But help me make a change
   that others might see.
Help me teach the deaf
   that they may hear
Your Heavenly Words
   without pain or fear.
Let me bring to You
   those who are lame,
And let them spiritually walk
   In Your Faithful Name.
The ones who can't speak?
   I'll teach them to pray,
So they can tell You things
   they've been wanting to say.
May You light the path
   that each of us face,
And deliver us up
   In your Glory and Grace.*

*By Michelle Palms. Copyright © 1988. Used by permission.

SEVEN

Silent Friends Sunday School

I will sing [sign] to the LORD all my life;
I will sing [sign] praise to my God as long as I
live.
May my meditation be pleasing to him,
as I rejoice in the LORD.

—PSALM 104:33–34

WELCOME TO *Silent Friends* Sunday school class, a special class of eight deaf people eager to learn God's Word.

This particular Sunday morning the topic is "worship," a concept often foreign to both deaf and hearing people. It is time to bring the class to order. I begin by blinking on and off the lights—the ultimate attention-getter at any deaf function. Joe, the president of the class, opens with prayer requests and announcements. This is a time for the participants to share the needs of their peers and the interests of the deaf community. Next on the agenda is Dorinne, the hospitality chairman, who leads in a few worship choruses. The mood begins to change as the class prepares their hearts for the morning's lesson.

I write the letters W-O-R-S-H-I-P on the board. Every person in the room immediately folds his or her right hand over the lefthand knuckles, drawing the hands toward oneself—signing the word "worship."

I ask in American Sign Language, *Means* [shrug]? ("What does it mean?") After a long pause, someone finally signs a response: *Don't know me, explain can't.* ("I don't know; I just can't explain it.")

Think how you would explain the concept of worship to your deaf Sunday school class. Webster's dictionary defines *worship* as "to have an intense or exaggerated admiration or devotion for; honor; to perform acts or have sentiments of worship."

I like the expression "perform acts" from the definition. For the purpose of this class, performing acts is exactly what I must do. I must throw all my inhibitions out the window. My goal is to show *visually* the meaning of worship. So . . .

I fall on my knees, imagining solitude. I begin flashing signs of praise for who God is: the one and only God, all-powerful (omnipotent), knowing everything (omniscient), Creator of all, and yet willing to forgive me, a sinner, through the sacrifice of his Son Jesus on the cross. I move into a simple praise song:

> Praise the name of Jesus
> Praise the name of Jesus
> He's my rock [*strength*]
> He's my fortress [*protector*]
> He's my deliverer [*savior*]
> In Him will I trust
> Praise the name of J-E-S-U-S.

I pray for God's forgiveness of my sins, listing them specifically. I then step out of my worship role and explain to the class that worship time is not a time to pray for God to "give me this and give me that," but a time to stop and listen and communicate with God one-on-one. Immediately a hand goes up, and Peter signs, *True, God understand sign language? God speak me how? Me deaf!* ("Do you really think God understands sign language? I mean, how can God speak to me? I'm deaf!")

Before I can lead Peter to a confirming Scripture passage, Faye looks to Peter and with conviction signs, *God deaf not, heart with-in convict.* ("God is not deaf; it's within our heart that he speaks to us.")

How true! Whether or not we speak with our voices, he always listens to our hearts.

I can see from the class members' expressions that enlightenment has begun. Heads are nodding; eyes have become alert. The Holy Spirit is present.

We turn in our Bibles to Isaiah 59:1–2. A volunteer signs the Scripture:

> Surely the arm of the LORD [the power of the Lord] is not too
>   short [is enough] to save,
>   nor his ear too dull to hear [he can hear you when you ask for
>   help].
> But your iniquities have separated you from your God;
>   your sins have hidden his face from you [he sees your sins],
>   so that he will not hear [he does not listen].

Means [shrug], *sometimes God deaf, same me?* Linda signs. ("You mean to tell me that God is deaf just like me?")

I am puzzled for a moment, then agree that although God hears prayers in any language, he can choose to ignore them when our unconfessed sin hinders communication with him. I realize then that, yes, God may adopt a hearing impairment in dealing with his people. How interesting!

Returning to the topic at hand, "worship," I show the class that the best example I have for worshiping methods is Jesus himself.

> In Luke 22:39–42 we read of Jesus' returning to his Father
> and seeking a secluded place to spend time alone communi-
> cating with him. I add that those secluded reunions were often
> held when the sun was just rising. For some of us, that's a
> goal for future achievement and a task yet to be conquered.
> In addition, the song of David in Psalm 5:3 emphasizes the
> benefits of early morning communion with the Lord:

> In the morning, O LORD, you hear my voice;
>   in the morning I lay my requests before you
>   and wait in expectation.

> To worship with consistency requires discipline and desire. We
> need an earnest hunger for a closer relationship with the Lord
> and the willingness to give him time, that precious commodity
> we think we have so little of. In reality, we have 168 hours
> every week to do whatever our heart desires. What do we do
> with those hours? What are the priorities in our everyday life?

The word *priority* arouses curiosity in the class. I write on the board "the things that are important to me" in random order

- Family
- Job
- Relationship with God

- Church
- Friends

and then continue.

> I usually spend most of my time with what's most important to me. Notice what is number one on my list. Striving to keep my priorities in a godly order is no easy task. I can certainly relate to what Paul says in Romans 7:18–19:
>
> > I have the desire to do what is good, but I cannot carry it out. For what I do is not the good I want to do; no, the evil I do not want to do—this I keep on doing.

From the positive headshakes, I feel the class is beginning to understand. To make sure, I ask two of them to write *their* priorities on the board and to be honest about them.

Mike	Mary
1. Bowling	1. Horses
2. Job	2. Job
3. Wife	3. School
4. Church	4. Deaf club

As I observe these deaf individuals' priorities, it dawns on me, "No wonder there is little or no desire to spend time alone with God. He is not even among their priorities!" So how can I introduce the class to this new concept of spending time alone with God and encourage them to make him a priority?

I emphasize that a person who has truly accepted Jesus Christ as Savior and Lord (a lesson taught numerous times in class) should strive for the following priorities:

1. God—our relationship with him through prayer and his relationship with us through his Word
2. Family—husband, wife, children
3. Church—ministry, fellowship
4. Job
5. Social Activities—deaf club, bowling

> These priorities are foreign to hearing and deaf people alike. We must strive constantly for a godly order in our everyday activities. With the Holy Spirit as our helper, we *can* be obedient in regard to godly priorities.

Cathie poses a question: *Me desire change life priorities, begin how?* ("I really desire to change my priorities, but how do I start?")

It happens to be the first day of a new month. I suggest reading from the Psalms or Proverbs each day of the month.

> Set aside at least ten minutes alone with God in the morning. Write down on paper three things you are thankful for along with names of friends and family who need prayer. Bring your lists to class next week to share. I urge the class to commit to one another and hold one another accountable.

I end the lesson with a hypothetical situation. We open our Bibles to Revelation 3:15. I set the scene for our future, face-to-face encounter with Jesus Christ. I call Mary forward and speak the words of Christ, asking her a crucial question: *Me (Jesus) allow you enter heaven why?* ("Why should I—Jesus—allow you to enter heaven?")

I draw Mary's attention to her list of priorities on the board. Mary agrees that she takes care of God's creation (her horses) and she does her yardwork faithfully. And she never misses a day of work and is a very dedicated student. I impress upon Mary that these are important responsibilities and she is to be commended for following through with her commitments; yet they should not be her ultimate priorities.

Resuming the viewpoint of Christ, I tell Mary that I left her on earth for a very important reason, namely, to tell others about me (Matt. 28:19). She is to proclaim my act of love (the Crucifixion) to all people (Luke 23). I want to share with her Revelation 3:15–16:

> "I know your deeds, that you are neither cold nor hot. I wish you were either one or the other! So, because you are luke-warm—neither hot nor cold—I am about to spit you out of my mouth."

I say in ASL, *I desire you enthusiastic or backslide, but you ride-fence [shrug], I cast you away.*

I emphasize that I am not the one saying this, but that God said it in his Word, the Bible. I urge the class to start this week to change their *priorities*—no longer an unknown term.

Faye signs enthusiastically, *First, obey God must!* ("It must be our utmost priority to obey God".) In unison the deaf class signs, *Amen!*

We close in prayer, on our knees.

As I leave the room and step into the autumn sunlight, I am filled with emotion. The breeze blowing against my face makes me think of Pentecost, when the Holy Spirit came from heaven like a rushing wind. I knew the Lord was present in that Sunday school room, using my hands to convey his message.

115

I recall each person's expression—the puzzled looks, heads nodding in agreement, hands flying with emotion, even the conviction I saw in their eyes. "This must be what a blessing is supposed to feel like, full and overflowing with thankfulness and praise to God for what he has done."

I had seen the beginnings of spiritual growth during that Sunday school hour. God's Word was sent forth living and active and sharper than any two-edged "sign," overcoming all the physical difficulties, piercing as far as the division of soul and spirit, joints and marrow, and able to judge the thoughts and intentions of the heart (Heb. 4:12). God's Word did not fall on "deaf" ears that day, but instead met eyes ready and eager to receive what God had for them. I was a tool for communicating the message in their own language, but the *connection* with those deaf people came from the Holy Spirit.

Teaching and working with deaf people fill me with inexpressible joy. Being able to lead a deaf person to a personal relationship with Christ is the ultimate blessing. I will never forget the time Ellen and I knelt together and signed a prayer of forgiveness and salvation. When I lifted my eyes and saw a tear running down her cheek, I thought to myself, "This is true ministry, one-on-one the way Jesus always intended! How precious, how special, oh, how right!"

I have not always done the teaching. Deaf people have taught me a great deal, especially about "honesty." Candidness is a common characteristic of deaf people. Once during a Bible study, the words *omniscience* and *omnipotent* were being examined. The class listened with awe as they learned that God knew their future and every thought in their mind. When I asked how they felt about that, a young man named Jeff immediately responded, *Me don't like, he nosey God, he business none!* ("I don't like it a bit; God's nosey and it's none of his business!")

I had to laugh inside. Sometimes that's how *I* feel! Jeff's honesty reminded me that I too need to deal truthfully with my feelings and thoughts. If I don't think God is being fair, then I have to express it, much as the psalmist David so often did. I was encouraged that day to look deep within, and I found a calloused heart in need of softening—thanks to Jeff.

COMMITTED TO SIGNING

I have related only a few of the blessings gained from my experiences with deaf people over the years. I am sure even more blessed experiences await you. James 1:25 says, "A doer of the work shall be blessed in his deed" (paraphrased).

Working with deaf people has included not only blessings, but also frustrations, tears, laughter, pain, anger, perplexity—all the realities of life. But through it all there has always been that joyous presence, with his promise never to leave me or forsake me.

Sign language is a part of me, and I am a part of sign language. I am committed. Is God asking this of you?

Ben Isham knew this challenge and wrote the following poem.

COMMITMENT

The sun its daily course has run,
And duties of the day seem done
So heart's adrift and free.
But You, blest Lord, with touch Divine
Lay'st claim upon these hands of mine
To work full-time for You.

My life, my all are Yours alone,
Your claims o'er me I humbly own,
Bow to Your sovereign will.
You do not want the swift nor strong
But those whose hearts to You belong,
Whom You can use Your way.

You break down, Lord, my stubborn will,
My restless spirit You can still.
So, Lord, I pray, now let
My eyes, my voice, my hands, my feet
Be ready for each need to meet
*As by Your Spirit led.**

*Ben Isham, a hearing-impaired minister and the author of *No Time to Lose,* went to be with the Lord August 19, 1985, but his burden and love for deaf people lives on. Copyright © 1981. Used by permission.

DEAFNESS

■ ■ ■

Born deaf
Silence surrounds me like walls
No music
No laughter

Brings difficulties for me to face
Places faults on my parents
Ashamed to accept
The way I am.

Clouds of patience
Fly around and around
Inside my body and its soul.
Suffers for the rest of my life.

But, inside me,
It's full of strengths
That doesn't let me
*Give up my life.**

*By Debra Cole. Used by permission of Gallaudet University.

EIGHT

Looking Ahead: A Deaf Pastor's Perspective

I do not consider myself yet to have taken hold of it. But one thing I do: forgetting what is behind and straining toward what is ahead, I press on.

—PHILIPPIANS 3:13

*T*HE TECHNIQUES and approaches to deaf work are changing. It is an exciting time for deaf people and those involved in deaf work. There is not only a concerted effort to evangelize deaf people, but a need to establish deaf congregations around the world.

With enhanced methods come new challenges, it is time to review our approaches to ministry and assess whether the spiritual needs of the deaf communities are currently being met. And if not, why not? I summon you to a new and stimulating challenge, to open your hearts and minds to new strategies and fresh ideas.

Pastor Samuel Marsh (deaf) and his wife, Brenda (hard of hearing), give vital perspective and helpful insights into the spiritual needs of deaf people today. I believe their comments give us direction in analyzing and evaluating the needs of the hearing-impaired people we seek to serve. What follows is the Marshes' perspective.

SOCIETY'S MISCONCEPTIONS

Society has had the idea that deaf people are incomplete and consequently it has often denied deaf people the rights of personhood. History has recorded humanity's prejudice and the deprivation that has resulted from it. For this reason, deaf people can rightly be considered oppressed. Now we are seeking to make the deaf people whole within their own culture, respecting them for who they are and what they can contribute to society and the church. We must remember that impairment is not to be equated with incompetence. Human uniqueness provides the opportunity to demonstrate God's love and power (1 Cor. 1:27; 2 Cor. 12:9).

At a recent DEAFWAY conference held at Gallaudet University, a statement was made that religion is not a part of the deaf culture or heritage. The reasoning is that religious work among the deaf has been so controlled and infiltrated by the hearing community that the deaf have not actually experienced their own worship of God; as a result, many claim that religion has no place in the deaf community. It is devastating to hear deaf leaders from around the world agreeing with this statement. What has the church done wrong? It is time to evaluate what we are doing and decide to whom we really need to minister: to ourselves, to those who work with deaf people, to the hearing congregation so often inspired by the beauty of interpretation, or to the deaf community.

A NEW CONCEPT: INDIGENOUS CHURCHES

It is well-accepted in international missions work that the most effective ministries use native speakers of an ethnic language group to reach out to their own people. Somehow this concept has not been seen as appropriate for the deaf community.

Today the concept of deaf people reaching deaf people is a trend that is slowly becoming widely accepted. Does this mean that hearing people should no longer minister in the deaf community? Of course not! We must remember that deaf people tend to gravitate toward others like them. Certain cultural "requirements" must be fulfilled for a hearing person to enter the deaf community for ministry. These conditions include seeking ways to meet the needs of both the deaf congregation and the deaf community rather than trying to force ill-fitting methods adopted from a hearing church. The hearing person must be willing to change and minister according to what works best for deaf people instead of doing what is most comfortable for the hearing congregation.

Consider, for example, the problem of hearing pastors who desire to speak while signing a message. Though this may be convenient for the preacher, it effectively prevents the use of clear, conceptual American Sign Language. It is impossible to use two different structures of language at the same time. The hearing pastor whose native language is English will continue to sign under the influence of that language as long as he chooses to vocalize. Communicating the message of Christ successfully is greatly hindered when the deaf congregation is forced to receive it in a "foreign language."

Deaf ministries in the past have tended not to be open to necessary change. The hearing person who has a burden for deaf ministry must be willing to lay aside "hearing life" and take on a "deaf life." Paul said, " I have become all things to all men so that by all possible means I might save some" (1 Cor. 9:22). Hearing people must be willing to immerse themselves in the deaf culture in order to present the gospel effectively.

The Indigenous Church Philosophy

The indigenous principle for churches is simply stated as "churches that are self-supporting, self-governing, and self-propagating." The philosophy works for the following reasons:

- Most important, the indigenous approach is a biblical approach. On the Day of Pentecost (Acts 2), God gave the apostles the ability to present the gospel in many languages so all could understand and receive. Paul fought hard to make the gospel available to people within their own culture. Likewise, we should enable deaf people to worship God in their own language and culture.
- A study was conducted among the deaf churches and interpreted ministries in one mainline denomination. The findings were astounding. Of all spiritual conversions among the deaf in this denomination, 90 percent came from the thirty deaf churches and only 10 percent from the two hundred interpreted ministries.

AWAKENING THE CHURCH

A group of deaf pastors and leaders at a recent ministry conference met with resistance from their hearing colleagues when they expressed their feelings that deaf people suffer oppression. Many times, hearing people are reluctant to believe that the church is guilty of injustice toward the deaf. In fact, deaf people have had no control over their education and have been discouraged from using their own language within their own culture. They have been given little or no leadership responsibility anywhere in the church.

Today we see a new boldness among deaf people who are seeking to participate fully in the life and worship of the body of Christ. Christian deaf leaders are gaining the confidence to speak out as they depend on the Holy Spirit to empower and direct their lives. We all—hearing and deaf—must pray that God will lead us through this transitional era in deaf work. Stubborn resistance to change will breed insecurity, feelings of intimidation, and resentment. This can in fact be seen today in situations like the protest at Gallaudet University in 1988.

Let us focus on ministering to the *felt needs* of deaf people. One hearing pastor in deaf ministry came to realize the weaknesses in his approach to deaf people as he sat at a dinner table and inquired of a hearing worker how to lead deaf home Bible studies. Suddenly he was aware that at the same table was a deaf man who been conducting such Bible studies for many years. The pastor directed his questions toward the deaf man and gained valuable insights. Because of this encounter, the pastor vowed that he would henceforth seek the advice of deaf people first in matters involving deaf ministry.

This change in direction marked a great stride forward in that church. For years the deaf members were not allowed to take leadership roles because they did not know how to lead. Now deaf leaders are being trained. Not surprisingly, that pastor is regarded by deaf leaders as "one of us."

OVERCOMING OBSTACLES

Since the mid-seventies we have observed an increase of young deaf and hearing adults responding to a "calling" from God to full-time ministry as evangelists, music ministers, youth directors, missionaries, pastors, teachers, and leaders in deaf churches.

A classic example is Severa, a deaf woman who was called to be a missionary to deaf people in 1978. At first she was told she lacked training, education, and finances, and—above all—her deafness was considered a hindrance. She did not give up, but instead persevered and prayed for five years, asking God to open a door to ministry for her. God heard her prayer, and Severa is now an extraordinary servant for the Lord.

Severa demonstrated a perseverance that graces her name. But she could not have acquired the necessary training alone. In his grace God provided a hearing woman who lived out John 15:13: "Greater love has no one than this, that a man lay down his life for his friends." This woman poured her life into training Severa to minister within her deaf culture. The Lord has continued to use this hearing woman as a role model for others in deaf work. In laying down her life for deaf people, she has now trained and enabled many young deaf and hearing adults for ministry. Her pioneer work brought on new and challenging concepts for future deaf work.

Samuel Marsh is one of the people whose lives have been indelibly touched by this hearing woman to minister in the deaf culture. Marsh relates:

In reflecting the Lord's calling, I remembered his affirmation in Scripture: John 21:15–18. Jesus questioned the depth of Peter's love for him. Three times Peter answered Jesus, and three times Jesus challenged him, saying, "Feed my sheep." These verses burdened me heavily. There are many deaf people who need a spiritual shepherd who loves Christ so much that he will lay down his life for the sheep—the deaf congregation. I was overwhelmed with the vision of my becoming a shepherd.

Another reaffirming Scripture text was Romans 10:14–15, which contains a question: "How can they hear without someone preaching to them?" I realized that deaf people must be given the message of Jesus Christ in the way they can "hear"—in their own language, ASL. To my mind it was like God "signing" to me, *They need a role-model pastor.* If I were willing to be trained and sent, God was willing and ready to do the sending. I then understood the responsibility I had as a deaf Christian to meet the needs of deaf people in my world. Deaf Opportunity Outreach (D.O.O.R.) provided me with specialized training and influenced my life to give me knowledge and confidence to be a shepherd.

In my own ministry, Marsh continues, I follow the philosophy that cultural groups have the right to be taught, worship, and serve God within their own linguistic and cultural contexts. An indigenous person is the most effective witness to others in any culture and language group.

Deaf people, properly motivated and trained, are the most effective witnesses to other deaf people. A properly motivated deaf church, growing under the positive leadership of a qualified pastor, can become a powerful spiritual force in the deaf community.

Therefore, my dear brothers [and sisters], stand firm. Let nothing move you. Always give yourselves fully to the work of the Lord, because you know that your labor in the Lord is not in vain. **—1 CORINTHIANS 15:58**

Afterword

■ ■ ■

REFLECTING ON nearly twenty years of involvement in deaf ministry, I praise God for what he has done. My role has changed from time to time as different needs have arisen. I began my work as an interpreter, and God used me even though I had little experience. Responsibilities increased steadily as time passed, and I found myself writing and teaching Sunday school lessons, teaching sign language classes, leading seminars, training and coordinating interpreters, arranging transportation and visitation and counseling—and other tasks.

Obviously I couldn't keep doing all these things for long. The deaf people I served needed to assume some of the responsibilities as the ministry grew. The more this happened, the more I saw the importance of my letting go and allowing them to gain leadership. So I worked myself out of many of my responsibilities.

Today I serve in a much different capacity in the local deaf community. The deaf congregation is now led by a deaf pastor, and they do almost everything for themselves. My role is to be a communication link between the hearing and deaf worlds. Occasionally I teach as a substitute, and I still enjoy discipling deaf women, praying for the church, sending notes of encouragement, and opening my home in hospitality.

My most recent deaf work is writing this book and sharing its contents at conferences and workshops. I am amazed to see God using me in these ways, for I consider myself an ordinary woman who started loving deaf people. If God can work as he has in me, he can work in you to minister to and with deaf people. A favorite Scripture verse has been an encouragement to me; let it be an encouragement to you:

He who began a good work in you will carry it on to completion until the day of Christ Jesus (Phil. 1:6).

Resources

■ ■ ■

References and General Resources

Bearden, C. Jr. *The Deaf Leader: A Leadership Manual for the Deaf.* Nashville: Southern Baptist Convention of the Deaf, 1986.
For more information on correspondence and other seminary extension courses on the Bible and ministry-related themes:
Seminary Extension Independent Study Institute
Southern Baptist Convention Building
901 Commerce Street / Suite 500
Nashville, TN 37203

Carder, S. *Ministering to the Deaf.* Sun Valley, Calif.: Grace Community Church, 1986.
13248 Roscoe Boulevard
Sun Valley, CA 91352

Daily Devotions for the Deaf
Deaf Missions
R.R. 2, Box 26
Council Bluffs, IA 51503

Deaf Evangelism. (A booklet available from General Assemblies of God Division of Home Missions, 1445 Boonville Avenue, Springfield, MO 65802.)

Deckworth, M. *Families of Handicapped Children: Helping Others in Crisis.* Elgin, Ill.: David C. Cook, 1988.

Ford, L. *A Primer for Teachers and Leaders.* Nashville: Broadman, 1963. (Learning made easy in graphic "picture book" style.)

_____. *A Sourcebook of Learning Activities.* Nashville: Broadman, 1984.

Herndon, C. *Lift Up Your Hands and Worship.* Lake Worth, Fla.: Best of Life Press, 1977.
2338 South Military Trail
Lake Worth, FL 33463

The Holy Bible: English Version for the Deaf. Grand Rapids: Baker, 1987. (Also available through Deaf Missions.)

Hughes, M. *A Master Plan for Disciplemaking.* Nashville: Sunday School Board of the Southern Baptist Convention, 1980.

Isham, B. *No Time to Lose: Understanding and Helping the Millions in the World of Silence.*

Voice from the Silence, Inc.
P.O. Box 182
Concord, CA 94522

Jeffries, M. *Deaf Workers' Handbook*. Hammond, Ind.: First Baptist Church, n.d..
Deaf Ministry
First Baptist Church
523 Sibley Street
Hammond, IN 46320

Lawrence, E. D. *Ministering to the Silent Minority: How to Develop a Church Ministry for the Deaf*. Springfield, Mo.: Gospel Publishing House, 1978.

Manual for Work with the Deaf. (A booklet available through Home Missions Board of the Southern Baptist Convention, 1350 Spring Street NW, Atlanta, GA 30309.)

Mears, H. M. *What the Bible Is All About: Teacher's Edition*. Ventura, Calif.: Regal, 1983. (Teacher's resource book.)

————. *What the Bible Is All About: Young Explorers*. Ventura, Calif.: Regal, 1986. (Student's resource book.)

Newman, Gene, and Joni Eareckson Tada. *All God's Children: Ministry to the Disabled*. Grand Rapids: Zondervan, Ministry Resources Library, 1981.

The New Testament: English Version for the Deaf. Grand Rapids: Baker, 1978. (Also available through Deaf Missions.)

Noe, H. L. *Starting a Ministry to the Deaf*. (A booklet available through Deaf Missions.)

Pentz, C. M. *Ministry to the Deaf*. Wheaton, Ill.: Tyndale House, 1978.

Rolfsrud, E. N. *One to One: Communicating the Gospel to the Deaf and Blind*. Minneapolis: Augsburg, 1961.

Tada, Joni Eareckson, and B. Singleton. *Friendship Unlimited: How You Can Help a Disabled Friend*. Wheaton, Ill.: Harold Shaw Publishers, 1987.

Tooney, S. K. *Mime Ministry*. Colorado Springs: Meriwether, n.d.
P.O. Box 7710
Colorado Springs, CO 80933

Werner, D. *Disabled Village Children*. Palo Alto, Calif.: Hesperian Foundation, 1987.
P.O. Box 1692
Palo Alto, CA 94302

Yount, William R. *Be Opened! An Introduction to Ministry with the Deaf*. Nashville: Broadman, 1976.

————. *I Can't / I'll Try*. 1978.

William R. Yount
403 Maple Street / Apt. 201
Falls Church, VA 22046

Secular Resources Relating to Deafness

Baker, C., and R. Battison. *Sign Language and the Deaf Community*. Silver Spring, Md.: National Association of the Deaf, 1980.

Bowe, F., and M. Sternberg. *I'm Deaf Too*. Silver Spring, Md.: National Association of the Deaf, 1973.

Gannon, J. *Deaf Heritage: A Narrative History of Deaf America*. Silver Spring, Md.: National Association of the Deaf, 1981.

Higgins, P., and J. Nash. *Understanding Deafness Socially*. Springfield, Ill.: Charles C. Thomas, 1987.

Humphries, T., and C. Padden. *Deaf in America: View from a Culture*. Cambridge: Harvard University Press, 1988.

Jacobs, L. M. *A Deaf Adult Speaks Out*. Washington, D.C.: Gallaudet College Press, 1980.

Lane, Harlan. *When the Mind Hears: A History of the Deaf*. New York: Random House, 1984.

Lucus, C. *The Sociolinguistics of the Deaf Community*. Washington, D.C.: Gallaudet University Press, 1989.

Ogden, Paul W., and Suzanne Lipsett. *The Silent Garden: Understanding the Hearing-Impaired Child*. Chicago: Contemporary Books, 1983.

Sacks, Oliver. *Seeing Voices: A Journey into the World of the Deaf*. Berkeley: University of California Press, 1989.

Spradley, T. S., and J. P. Spradley. *Deaf Like Me*. New York: Random House, 1978.

Walker, L. A. *A Loss for Words: The Story of Deafness in a Family*. New York: Harper & Row, 1986.

Wilcox, S. *American Deaf Culture: An Anthology*. Silver Spring, Md.: Linstok Press, 1989.

Sign Language and Communication Resources

Baker, C., and C. Padden. *American Sign Language: A Look at Its History, Structure, and Community*. Silver Spring, Md.: T. J. Publishers, 1978.

Bearden, C. *Handbook for Religious Interpreters for the Deaf*. Atlanta: Home Mission Board of the Southern Baptist Convention, 1975.

Bearden, C., and J. Potter. *Manual of Religious Signs*. Atlanta: Home Mission Board of the Southern Baptist Convention, 1973.

Christian Education and Hearing Impaired Children.
Christian Education and Hearing Impaired Adolescents.
Christian Education and Hearing Impaired Adults.
Kits prepared by the Task Force on Educational Ministry and Hearing Impaired Persons. Available through Division of Education and Ministry, National Council of Churches of Christ, 475 Riverside Drive, New York, NY 10027.

Cokley, D., and C. Baker. *American Sign Language: A Student Text.* Silver Spring, Md.: T. J. Publishers, 1980.

Costello, E. *Religious Signing: The New Comprehensive Guide for All Faiths.* New York: Bantam, 1986.

_____. *Signing: How to Speak with Your Hands.* New York: Bantam, 1983.

Decker, L. *Facilitating Manual Communication for Interpreters, Students, and Teachers.* Silver Spring, Md.: National Association of the Deaf, 1978.

Fant, Louie J. *The American Sign Language Phrase Book.* Chicago: Contemporary Books, 1983.

Greenberg, J. *In This Sign.* New York: Avon Books, 1970.

Joslin, G. *Let's Sign: A Sign Language Training Guide for the Church.* Richmond: Multi-Media Evangelism, 1982.
South Providence Road
Richmond, VA 23236

Lawrence, E. D. *Sign Language Made Simple: A Complete Manual for Learning Sign Language in Sentence Form.* Springfield, Mo.: Gospel Publishing House, 1979.

O'Rourke, T. J. *A Basic Course in Manual Communication.* Silver Spring, Md.: National Association of the Deaf, 1973.

Rice, C. *Sign Language for Everyone.* Nashville: Thomas Nelson, 1977.

Riekehoff, L. *The Joy of Signing.* Springfield, Mo.: Gospel Publishing House, 1978.

_____. *Talk to the Deaf.* Springfield, Mo.: Gospel Publishing House, 1963. (A manual of approximately 1,000 signs used by deaf North Americans.)

Royster, Mary A. *Games and Activities for Sign Language Classes.* Silver Spring, Md.: National Association of the Deaf, 1974.

Solow, S. *Sign Language Interpreting: A Basic Resource Book.* Silver Spring, Md.: National Association of the Deaf, 1981.

Publications and Newsletters

Information on publications marked by an (*) was provided by the National Information Center on Deafness, Gallaudet College.

800 Florida Avenue NE
Washington, DC 20002
(202) 651-5109 (voice)
(202) 651-5976 (TDD)

American Annals of the Deaf. (Published five times a year).
KDES - PAS #6
800 Florida Avenue NE
Washington, DC 20002

*American Athletic Association of the Deaf Newsletter
Cole Zolauf, Editor
1313 Tanforan Drive
Lexington, KY 40502

The Branding Iron
Bill Rice Ranch
Murfreesboro, TN 37130
(813) 689-5671

Communication Service for the Deaf (Newsletter available.)
3520 Galeway Lane
Sioux Falls, SD 57106

DCARA
Deaf Counseling, Advocacy, and Referral Agency
125 Parrott Street
San Leandro, CA 94577

*The Deaf American
Muriel Horton-Strassler, Editor
National Association of the Deaf
814 Thayer Avenue
Silver Spring, MD 20910

Deaf Christian Times
Ken Davis Ministries
P.O. Box 41442
Sacramento, CA 95841

Deaf Life
c/o MSM Productions, Ltd.
Box 63083
Market Place Mall
Rochester, NY 14623-6383

Deaf USA Newspaper
Eye Festival Communications
1530 N. Gower Street, Suite 201
Hollywood, CA 90028

*The Endeavor
    Jacqueline Z. Mendelsohn, Editor
    American Society for Deaf Children
    814 Thayer Avenue
    Silver Spring, MD 20910

*The Frat
    National Fraternal Society of the Deaf
    1300 W. Northwest Highway
    Mt. Prospect, IL 60056

*Gallaudet Alumni Newsletter
    Jack R. Gannon, Editor
    Gallaudet College
    800 Florida Avenue NE
    Washington, DC 20002

Gallaudet Bookstore Catalog
    Kendall Green
    P.O. Box 300
    Washington, DC 20002
    (202) 651-5000

*Gallaudet Today
    Jack R. Gannon, Managing Editor
    Gallaudet College
    800 Florida Avenue NE
    Washington, DC 20002

His Hands Newsletter
    California Southern Baptist Deaf Ministry
    2091 Weston Circle
    Camarillo, CA 93010
    (805) 484-3936 (voice/TDD)

Joni & Friends Newsletter
    P.O. Box 3333
    Agoura Hills, CA 91301
    (818) 707-5664 (voice)
    (818) 707-7004 (TDD)

*Journal of Rehabilitation of the Deaf
    Glenn T. Lloyd, Editor
    American Deafness & Rehabilitation Association
    814 Thayer Avenue
    Silver Spring, MD 20910

*Junior NAD Newsletter
    Junior National Association of the Deaf, Branch Office
    455 N. Pennsylvania Street / Suite 804
    Indianapolis, IN 46204

Let's Sign Catalog
    4203 West Tilden Street
    Springfield, MO 65802
    (417) 864-8221 (voice/TDD)

NAD Bookstore Catalog
    814 Thayer Avenue
    Silver Spring, MD 20910
    (301) 587-1788

*NAD Broadcaster
    Muriel Horton-Strassler, Editor
    National Association of the Deaf
    814 Thayer Avenue
    Silver Spring, MD 20910

*Newsounds (Newsletter)
    Genie Doggett, Editor
    Alexander Graham Bell Association for the Deaf
    3417 Volta Place NW
    Washington, DC 20007

*NTID Focus
    Marcia Dugan, Editor
    National Technical Institute for the Deaf
    One Lomb Memorial Drive
    Rochester, NY 14623

SHHH Magazine: Self Help for Hard of Hearing People
    7800 Wisconsin Avenue
    Bethesda, MD 20814

Signing
    Mennonite Board of Missions, Deaf Ministries
    Box 370
    Elkhart, IN 46515-0370

*Silent News
    Walter Schulman, Editor
    P.O. Box 584
    Paramus, NJ 07652

Together
    Baptist General Convention of Texas
    Church Ministries Section / Suite 1013

Baptist Building
Dallas, TX 75201-3355

*Volta Review (Journal)
Richard Kretschmer, Editor
Alexander Graham Bell Association for the Deaf
3417 Volta Place NW
Washington, DC 20007

*The World Around You
Cathy Carroll, Editor
MSSD Box 5N
Gallaudet College
800 Florida Avenue NE
Washington, DC 20002

Christian Resources

The organizations listed are sources for materials relating to Christian education of deaf people.

The Assemblies of God
1445 Boonville Avenue
Springfield, MO 65802

Bill Rice Ranch
Murfreesboro, TN 37129

Boyce Bible School
2825 Lexington Road
Louisville, KY 40280

(One of the first schools in the U.S. to teach theological courses in sign language.)
Contact: David Q. Byrd
For prospective students: (502) 897-4617
For information: Southern Baptist Theological Seminary (502) 897-4011

Boys' Town National Institute for Communicational Disorders
555 N. 30th Street
Omaha, NE 68154

Catholic Office of the Deaf
155 E. Superior
Chicago, IL 60611
(312) 751-8370 (voice/TDD)

Celebrant Singers
P.O. Box 1416
Visalia, CA 93279
(209) 627-4000

(An international outreach using music and sign language interpretation.)

Child Evangelism Fellowship
    17310 S. Woodruff Avenue
    Bellflower, CA 90706

Christ for the Nations
    P.O. Box 24910
    Dallas, TX 75224

Christian Deaf Fellowship
    12800 Woodruff Avenue
    Downey, CA 90242

Central Bible College
    Springfield, MO 65803
    Contact: Edgar Lawrence

Deaf International Bible College
    800 South 10th Street
    Suite 5
    Minneapolis, MN 55404
    (612) 332-2081 (voice/TDD)

Deaf Ministries Worldwide
    P.O. Box 985
    Sulphur, OK 73086

Deaf Missions
    R.R. 2 / Box 26
    Council Bluffs, IA 51503

Deaf Missions/West Coast Office
    Crossroads Christian Church
    1775 South Main
    Corona, CA 91720
    (714) 279-7606
    (714) 352-0242

    (Deaf Missions publishes a catalog of Bible Visuals for the Deaf and materials about deafness [available on request] and also offers an extension class program.)

Deaf Opportunity Outreach (D.O.O.R.)
    Vesta Bice, Director
    P.O. Box 1327
    Louisville, KY 40201
    (502) 635-1700

Deaf Outreach Inc.
811 Wealthy Street
Grand Rapids, MI 49506

Deaf Prison Ministry
Robin Shifflett
P.O. Box 1635
Hawaiian Gardens, CA 90716
(213)860-0206 (TDD)

Ephphatha Services for the Deaf and Blind
American Lutheran Church
P.O. Box 713
Sioux Falls, SD 57101

Episcopal Conference of the Deaf
Executive Secretary
556 Zinnia Lane
Birmingham, AL 35215

Home Mission Board of the Southern Baptist Convention
Carter Bearden, Deaf Ministry Consultant
1350 Spring Street NW
Atlanta, GA 30367-5601

Joni and Friends
P.O. Box 3333
Agoura Hills, CA 91301
(818) 707-5664

Lutheran Church, Missouri Synod
Board of Missions
Ministry to the Deaf
1333 South Kirkwood Road
St. Louis, MO 63122
(314) 965-9917 ext. 321

National Council of Churches
Task Force on the Hearing Impaired
Division of Education and Ministry
475 Riverside Drive
New York, NY 10027

Operation Sound
1605 Elizabeth Street
Pasadena, CA 91104
(818) 797-7037 (TDD)

Presbyterian Church, U.S.
Division of National Missions
341 Ponce de Leon Avenue NE
Atlanta, GA 30308

St. Paul Technical Institute
    235 Marshall Avenue
    St. Paul, MN 55102

United Church of Canada
    Division of Mission in Canada
    85 St. Clair Avenue East
    Toronto, Ontario 44T IM8

United Methodist Church Network of Ministries with the Deaf
    Division of Global Ministries
    Third Floor
    475 Riverside Drive
    New York, NY 10027

Voice from the Silence, Inc.
    P.O. Box 182
    Concord, CA 94522
    (415) 686-3966 (voice/TDD)

Western Evangelical Seminary
    4200 S.E. Jennings Avenue
    Portland, OR 97222

Deaf Churches, Synagogues, and Religious Associations

*American Bible Society
    1865 Broadway
    New York, NY 10023
    (212) 581-7400

*American Ministries to the Deaf, Inc.
    7564 Browns Mill Road
    Kauffman Station
    Chambersburg, PA 17201
    (717) 375-2610

*Catholic Charities Office for the Handicapped: Deaf Division
    191 Joralmon Street
    Brooklyn, NY 11201
    (718) 596-5500

*Catholic Deaf Apostolate
    243 Steele Road
    West Hartford, CT 06117
    (203) 523-7530

*Christian Record Braille Foundation, Inc.
    Deaf Services Department
    444 S. 52nd Street

Lincoln, NE 68506
(402) 488-0981

*Christian Reformed Church Committee on Disability Concerns
2850 Kalamazoo Avenue, SE
Grand Rapids, MI 49560

Directory of Southern Baptist Churches Ministering to the Deaf
Home Mission Board, Southern Baptist Convention
1350 Spring Street NW
Atlanta, GA 30367

*Evangelical Lutheran Church of America
Division of Social Ministry Organizations
8765 West Higgins Road
Chicago, IL 60631
(312) 380-3700

*Episcopal Conference of the Deaf
All Souls for the Deaf
Box 27459
Philadelphia, PA 19150

*Episcopal Conference of the Deaf
1210 Locust Street
St. Louis, MO 63101
(314) 421-2685 (voice/TDD)

First Presbyterian Church of Hollywood
1760 North Gower Street
Hollywood, CA 90028
(213) 463-7161 (voice)
(213) 204-3570 (TDD)

*General Council of the Assemblies of God
Division of Home Missions
Ministries to the Deaf
1445 Boonville Avenue
Springfield, MO 65802
(417) 862-2781

*Gospel Ministries for the Deaf
4200-A S.E. Jennings Avenue
Portland, OR 97627
(503) 393-5153

*International Catholic Deaf Association
814 Thayer Avenue
Silver Spring, MD 20910
(301) 588-4009 (TDD)

*International Lutheran Deaf Association
    1333 S. Kirkwood Road
    St. Louis, MO 63122
    (314) 965-9917 ext. 321

International Outreach to the Deaf
    P.O. Box 1304
    San Jose, CA 95109-1304
    (408) 287-2229 (voice/TDD)
    Contact: Vesta Bice

Jewish Big Brothers for Deaf and Hard of Hearing Children
    11646 W. Pico Blvd.
    Los Angeles, CA 90064
    (213) 445-4200 (voice)
    (213) 477-8770 (TDD)

*Mennonite Board of Missions
    Office of Deaf Ministries
    P.O. Box 370
    Elkhart, IN 46515
    (219) 294-7523 ext. 286

*National Catholic Office of the Deaf
    814 Thayer Avenue
    Silver Spring, MD 20910
    (301) 587-7992 (voice/TDD)

*National Congress of Jewish Deaf
    4960 Sabbal Palm Blvd. / Bldg. 7, Apt. 207
    Tamarac, FL 33319

*National Council of the Churches of Christ in the U.S.A.
    Task Force on Hearing Impairments
    Division of Education and Ministry
    475 Riverside Drive / Rm. 706
    New York, NY 10115
    (212) 870-2042

*Office of Deaf Ministries
    National Division
    Board of Global Ministries of the United Methodist Church
    475 Riverside Drive
    New York, NY 10115
    (212) 870-3909

Preacher Training Program for the Deaf
    Sunset School of Preaching
    3723 34th Street
    Lubbock, TX 79410

(806) 792-5191 (voice)
Contact: Bob Anderson and Hollis Maynard

*Presbyterian Church (U.S.A.)
Office of Social Welfare
475 Riverside Drive, Rm. 1268
New York, NY 10115
(212) 870-2043

*Southern Baptist Convention
John Cooper, Consultant
Special Ministries
Sunday School Board
127 Ninth Avenue, North
Nashville, TN 37234
(615) 251-2762

Southern Baptist General Convention of California
Howard Burkhart, Consultant
678 East Shaw Avenue
Fresno, CA 93710
(209) 229-9533

*United Methodist Church
General Board of Global Ministries
475 Riverside Drive / Room 334
New York, NY 10115
(212) 870-3835

Secular Resources Relating to the Hearing Impaired

The organizations listed are sources of general information relating to the
hearing impaired.

Alexander Graham Bell Association for the Deaf
3417 Volta Place NW
Washington, DC 20007
(202) 337-5220

*American Athletic Association of the Deaf
10604 E. 95th Street Terrace
Kansas City, MO 64134

*American Deafness and Rehabilitation Association
P.O. Box 55369
Little Rock, AR 72225
(501) 663-4617 (voice/TDD)

Association of Parents of the Deaf
814 Thayer Avenue
Silver Spring, MD 20910

California School for the Deaf, Fremont
    39350 Gallaudet Drive
    Fremont, CA 94538

*Convention of American Instructors of the Deaf
    P.O. Box 2163
    Columbia, MD 21045

Council of Organizations Serving the Deaf
    Wilds Lake Village Green
    Columbia, Maryland 21044

Deafness Research and Training Center
    New York University
    80 Washington Square East / Room 51
    New York, NY 10003

*Deafness Research Foundation
    9 East 38th Street
    New York, NY 10016
    (212) 684-6556 (voice)
    (212) 684-6559 (TDD)

*Deaf Pride Inc.
    1350 Potomac Avenue, SE
    Washington, DC 20003
    (202) 675-6700 (voice)/TDD)

Gallaudet College
    Kendall Green, NE
    Washington, DC 20002

Greater Los Angeles Council on Deafness, Inc. (GLAD)
    616 S. Westmoreland Avenue / 2nd Floor
    Los Angeles, CA 90005
    (213) 383-2220

*House Ear Institute
    256 South Lake
    Los Angeles, CA 90057
    (213) 483-4431 (voice)
    (213) 484-2642 (TDD)

*John Tracy Clinic
    806 West Adams Blvd.
    Los Angeles, CA 90007
    (213) 748-5481 (voice)
    (213) 747-2924 (TDD)

National Association of the Deaf (NAD)
 814 Thayer Avenue
 Silver Spring, MD 20910
 (301) 587-1788

*National Center for Law and the Deaf
 Gallaudet University
 800 Florida Avenue NE
 Washington, DC 20002
 (202) 651-5373 (voice/TDD)

National Center on Deafness (NCOD)
 California State University at Northridge (CSUN)
 Northridge, CA 91330
 (818) 885-2611 (voice/TDD)

*National Information Center on Deafness
 Gallaudet University
 800 Florida Avenue NE
 Washington, DC 20002
 (800) 672-6720 ext. 5051 (voice)
 ext. 5052 (TDD)

National Technological Institute for the Deaf (NTID)
 One Lomb Memorial Drive
 P.O. Box 9887
 Rochester, New York 14623
 (716) 475-6400 (voice)
 (716) 475-2181 (TDD)

*National Theatre of the Deaf
 Chester, CT 06412
 (203) 526-4971 (voice)
 (203) 526-4974 (TDD)

*Registry of Interpreters for the Deaf (RID)
 1 Metro Square
 51 Monroe Street / Suite 1107
 Rockville, MD 20850
 (301) 279-0555

San Francisco State University
 Deafness Rehabilitation Training Project
 School of Education
 1600 Holloway Avenue
 San Francisco, CA 94132
 (415) 338-1333 (voice)
 (415) 338-7869 (TDD)

*TRIPOD
>   955 North Alfred Street
>   Los Angeles, CA 90069
>   (213) 656-4904 (voice/TDD)

Insight into Indigenous Churches

American Mosaic Series of the Southern Baptist Home Mission Board
>   "Deaf Testimony"
>   America's Ethnicity
>   1989 Component
>   1-800-634-2462

Carter Bearden, Sr.
>   c/o Home Mission Board
>   Language Church Extension Division
>   1350 Spring Street NW
>   Atlanta, GA 30367-5601
>
>   (The paper "A Deaf Church" may be obtained from this national ethnic missionary at the stated address.)

*Deaf Opportunity Outreach (D.O.O.R.)
>   P.O. Box 1327
>   Louisville, KY 40201
>   (502) 635-1700
>
>   (Consulting service to planting deaf churches.)

Visual Resources

Christian and nonreligious closed captioned movies and video tapes.

American Culture: "The Deaf Perspective" (Four-part series.)
>   Friends of SFPL
>   Video Account
>   c/o Special Media Services
>   San Francisco Public Library
>   Civic Center
>   San Francisco, CA 94102

The Caption Center
>   Boston: 125 Western Avenue
>   Boston, MA 02134
>   (617) 492-9225 (voice/TDD)
>
>   New York: 231 East 55th Street
>   New York, NY 10022
>   (212) 223-4930 (voice)
>   (212) 223-5117 (TDD)
>
>   Los Angeles: 6255 Sunset Blvd. /Suite 723
>   Los Angeles, CA 90028

143

(213) 465-7616 (voice)
(213) 465-6818 (TDD)

Captioned Films for the Deaf
5000 Park Street North
St. Petersburg, FL 33709
(800) 237-6213 (voice/TDD)

(Write for an application and free catalog of movies available.)

Catalog of Captioned Educational Video Tapes
National Technical Institute for the Deaf
Division of Public Affairs / Dept. C
One Lomb Memorial Drive
P.O. Box 9887
Rochester, NY 14623-0887
(716) 475-6824 (voice/TDD)

Christian Captioned Films
811 Wealthy Street, SE
Grand Rapids, MI 49506

(Send for information and current list of titles.)

Deaf Video Communications of America, Inc.
4624 Yackley Avenue
Lisle, IL 60532
(312) 964-0909 (TTY)

Filmstrips with Captions
Concordia Publishing House
Audiovisuals Media
3558 S. Jefferson Street
St. Louis, MO 63118

(List of titles available.)

"Jesus" Sign Language Translation
Distributed by:
Deaf Missions
R.R. 2 / Box 26
Council Bluffs, Iowa 51503
(712) 322-5493 (voice/TDD)

(Perhaps the most historically accurate film ever made about the life of Christ, now available with sign language insert. Available for rental or purchase.)

Let's Sign (Sign language videos and catalog.)
4203 W. Tilden Street
Springfield, MO 65802

(417) 864-8221 (voice/TDD)
Contact: Lorene and George Joslin

Living Lessons from the Bible and *The Bible in A.S.L.* (Omega Project)
c/o Deaf Missions
R.R. 2 / Box 26
Council Bluffs, IA 51503
(712) 322-5493 (voice/TDD)

Media Services and Captioned Films
BEH, V.S. Office of Education
Seventh and D Streets
Washington, DC 20202

(Captioned films may be obtained free of charge.)

Multi-Media Evangelism, Inc.
1335 S. Providence Road
Richmond, VA 23236
(804) 276-9083
Contact: Howard Baldwin

National Captioning Institute, Inc. (NCI)
5203 Leesburg Pike
Falls Church, VA 22041
(703) 998-2416
(703) 998-2400 (TTY)
Contact: Don Thieme

National Captioning Institute, Inc.
1443 Beachwood Drive
Hollywood, CA
(213) 469-7000 (voice/TTY)

A Video Guide to the Basics of Sign Language
Crown Publishers, Inc.
Distributed by:
Crown Video
225 Park Avenue South
New York, NY 10003

Sign Language and Finger-Spelling Computer Programs

CAV-ASL (Computerized Animated Vocabulary of American Sign Language)
Microtech Consulting Company, Inc.
909 West 23rd Street
P.O. Box 521
Cedar Falls, IA 50613
Information: (319) 277-6648

Media and Entertainment Resources

Hey Listen!
> *A subsidiary of Visual Communication Service, Inc.*
> *36 St. Paul Street, Suite 104/108*
> *Rochester, NY 14604-1308*

The Meeting Place
> *Entertainment and Consumer Network*
> *12228 Venice Blvd. / Suite 349*
> *Los Angeles, CA 90064*
> *(213) 204-6006 (voice)*
> *(213) 204-3570 (TDD)*

Telecommunication Device Information

Harris Communications
> *3255 Hennepin Avenue / Suite 55*
> *Minneapolis, MN 55408*
> *1-800-825-6758 (voice/TDD)*

Weitbrecht Communications, Inc.
> *2656 29th Street / Suite 205*
> *Santa Monica, CA 90405*
> *(213) 452-8613 (voice)*
> *(213) 452-5460 (TDD)*

Krown Research
> *10371 West Jefferson Boulevard*
> *Culver City, CA 90232*
> *(213) 839-0181 (in California)*
> *(800) 833-4968 (outside California)*

GA-SK
> *Telecommunications for the Deaf, Inc.*
> *814 Thayer Avenue*
> *Silver Spring, MD 20910*
>
> *(A publication for telecommunication users.)*

Bibliography

■ ■ ■

Baker, Charlotte, and Carol Padden. *American Sign Language: A Look at Its History, Structure, and Community*. Silver Spring, Md.: T. J. Publishers, 1978.

Bice, Vesta. "Development of Deaf Choirs." Houston, Tex.: D.O.O.R., 1984.

Bice, Vesta, and Severa Trevino. "Dynamics of Deaf Culture." Wheaton, Ill.: Congress on the Church and the Disabled (July 1988).

Byron, Burnes B. "Who Are the Deaf?" *American Annals of the Deaf* 103, no. 2 (March 1958).

Carder, Stan. *Ministering to the Deaf*. Sun Valley, Calif.: Grace Community Church, 1986.

Cokley, Dennis, and Charlotte Baker. *American Sign Language: A Student Text*. Silver Spring, Md.: T.J. Publishers, 1980.

Engstrom, Ted W. *The Pursuit of Excellence*. Grand Rapids: Zondervan, 1982.

Hotchkiss, David. *Demographic Aspects of Hearing Impairment: Questions and Answers*. Washington, D.C.: Gallaudet University, 1987.

Isham, Ben. *No Time to Lose*. Concord, Calif.: Deaf Ministries International, 1981.

Johnson, Meriam. "The Expectations of an Interpreter." Conference handout, 1968.

Joslin, George B. *Manual for Work with the Deaf*. Atlanta: Home Mission Board of the Southern Baptist Convention, 1983.

Kanda, Jan. "Ideas for a Total Ministry." Amarillo, Tex.: Conference address, 1976.

Kanda, Jan H., and Jerry Seale. *Miss Lillian*. Arlington, Tex.: Deaf Ministry Services, 1974.

King, Duane. "Serving with Persons Who Are Deaf." Council Bluffs, Iowa: Deaf Missions, 1988.

Lawrence, Edgar D. *Ministering to the Silent Minority: How to Develop a Church Ministry for the Deaf*. Springfield, Mo.: Gospel Publishing House, 1978.

MacDonald, Gail. *High Call, High Privilege*. Wheaton, Ill.: Tyndale House, 1986.

National Information Center on Deafness. Washington, D.C.: Gallaudet University, 1987.

Newman, Gene, and Joni Eareckson Tada. *All God's Children.* Grand Rapids, MI: Zondervan Publishing House, Ministry Resources Library, 1981.

Noe, Harold L. *Starting a Ministry to the Deaf.* Council Bluffs, Iowa: Deaf Missions, 1986.

Pentz, Croft M. *Ministry to the Deaf.* Wheaton, Ill.: Tyndale House, 1978.

Price, James F. *Beginning a Work for the Deaf.* Council Bluffs, Iowa: Deaf Missions, 1982.

Ratheal, Melvin C. "The Interpreter and the Church Staff." Tucson, Ariz.: Conference for Work with the Deaf, Glorieta Baptist Assembly, 1968.

Riekehof, Lottie L. "General Principles in Religious Interpreting." Portland, Maine: Workshop for the Training of Interpreters, 1965.

Sacks, Oliver. *Seeing Voices: A Journey into the World of the Deaf.* Berkeley: University of California Press, 1989.

Schein, Jerome D. "The Deaf Community," in *Hearing and Deafness,* eds. Hollowell Davis and Richard Silverman. New York: Holt, Rinehart and Winston, 1978.

Schmidt, Henry J. "Moving Beyond the Four Walls," in *Christian Leader* 51, no. 20 (1988): 4–6.

Solow, Newman S. *Sign Language Interpreting.* Silver Spring, MD: A Publication of the National Association of the Deaf, 1981.

Tada, Joni Eareckson. *Friendship Unlimited.* Wheaton, IL: Harold Shaw Publishers, 1987.

Werner, David. *Disabled Village Children: A Guide for Community Health Workers, Rehabilitation Workers, and Families.* Palo Alto, CA: The Hesperian Foundation, 1987.

Notes

■ ■ ■

Chapter 1 – What Is Deafness?

1. Edgar D. Lawrence, *Ministering to the Silent Minority: How to Develop a Ministry for the Deaf* (Springfield, Mo.: Gospel Publishing House, 1980).

Chapter 2 — The Deaf Community

1. Harlan Lane, *When the Mind Hears: A History of the Deaf* (New York: Random House, 1984).

2. Oliver Sacks, *Seeing Voices: A Journey Into the World of the Deaf* (Berkeley: University of California Press, 1989), 138.

3. Ibid. See pages 21–29.

Chapter 3 — Calling the Church to Deaf Ministry

1. John Fischer, *Real Christians Don't Dance!* (Minneapolis: Bethany House, 1988), 37–39.

Chapter 4 — The Church Intepreter: God's Messenger

1. Croft M. Pentz, *Ministry to the Deaf* (Wheaton, Ill.: Tyndale House, 1978), 10–12.

2. Meriam Johnson, "The Expectations of an Interpreter" (N.p.: Conference handout, 1968).

3. Jan Kanda, "Ideas for a Total Ministry" (Amarillo, Tex.: Conference handout, 1976).

Chapter 5 — Sign to the Lord a New Song

1. Vesta Bice, *Development of Deaf Choirs: The Art of Making Music Visual* (Houston: D.O.O.R., 1984).

2. William E. Davis, "Suggestions for Interpreting Church Music," 1968.

3. Ibid.

4. Jerome Schein, *Speaking the Language of Sign: The Art and Science of Sign Language* (Garden City, N.Y.: Doubleday, 1984), 144–45.

Chapter 6 — Faith Comes by Seeing . . .

1. Lou Fant, *The American Sign Language Phrase Book* (Chicago: Contemporary Books, 1983), 1–3.

2. Ted W. Engstrom, *The Pursuit of Excellence* (Grand Rapids: Zondervan, 1982), 75.

3. A videotape companion to this book is available for your church, including basic conversational phrases, signed vocabulary, and conceptually signed music. Ordering information can be obtained from the following:

A Guide to Deaf Ministry
C/O Deaf Missions
R.R. 2 / Box 26
Council Bluffs, IA 51503
(712) 322-5493

If you desire information on the National Christian Interpreter's Conference sponsored by Joni and Friends, or if you would like to have me conduct a seminar at your church, please write:

DeAnn Sampley, Professor
Bakersfield College
1801 Panorama Drive
Bakersfield, CA 93305
(805) 395-4404

Index of Signs

■ ■ ■

Words and phrases in italic type are used in a context, that is, in a sentence.

153

SONGS AND SCRIPTURE IN TRANSLATION